Bread Machine Baking
for Better Health

Check your machine's instruction booklet to make sure your machine can bake whole grain breads. Some machines on the market today are equipped to make only lighter, white breads. If you bake whole grain breads in this type of machine, you'll eventually wear down the motor.

Bread Machine Baking
for Better Health

Delicious Bread Recipes
for Brimming Good Health

Maureen B. Keane
Daniella Chace

PRIMA HEALTH
A Division of Prima Publishing

PRIMA HEALTH and colophon are trademarks of Prima Communications, Inc.

Library of Congress Cataloging-in-Publication Data

Keane, Maureen.
    Bread machine baking for better health : delicious bread recipes for brimming good health / Maureen B. Keane and Daniella Chace.
        p. cm.
    Includes index.
    ISBN 1-55958-419-X
    ISBN 0-7615-1442-2
    1. Bread—Theraputic use.   2. Cookery (Bread).   I. Chace, Daniella.   II. Title.
RM258.K43 1994
613.2'6—dc20   93-35452
                                                                                      CIP

    00 01 HH 10 9 8 7 6 5 4 3
Printed in the United States of America

How to Order

Single copies may be ordered from Prima Publishing, 3000 Lava Ridge Court, Roseville, CA 95661; telephone (800) 632-8676. Quantity discounts are also available. On your letterhead, include information concerning the intended use of the books and the number of books you wish to purchase.

Visit us online at www.primalifestyles.com

To Lori Silverstein, who lit the fire under this project and who has been a major influence in our professional development.

CONTENTS

CHAPTER 1

In Celebration of Bread: The Role of Bread in the American Diet 1

CHAPTER 2

The Anatomy of Digestion 7

CHAPTER 3

Bread, Fiber, and Prevention 15

CHAPTER 4

Bread, Fiber, and Disease   25

CHAPTER 5

Bread, Dough, and Bread Machines   31

CHAPTER 6

Basic Breads   41

CHAPTER 7

Gluten-Restricted, and Wheat-, Rye-, Oat-, and Barley-Free Bread   58

CHAPTER 8

High-Fiber Breads   79

CHAPTER 9

High-Protein Breads   99

CHAPTER 10

Lactose-Free Breads   118

CHAPTER 11

Low-Fat, Cholesterol-Free, and Egg-Free Breads   135

CHAPTER 12

Low-Sodium and Low-Salt Breads 153

CHAPTER 13

Milk-Free Breads 171

CHAPTER 14

Wheat-Free Breads   189

Acknowledgments

To John, who bought me pizza when I could no longer look at bread.

A big thank you to LaMar Harrington for the use of her beautiful test kitchen and Chrysler Harrington for being our number-one bread critic. Just watching him enjoy each new bread recipe was an inspiration.

To our dear friends Merrilee and Nuria Gomez for your weekends of assistance on recipe development.

To a wonderful friend, Frances Albrecht, for delivering studies and books and assisting in many edits of nutrition text.

Thank you to Daniel Kennedy for the graphic illustrations in this text.

Bread Machine Baking
for Better Health

CHAPTER 1

In Celebration of Bread: The Role of Bread in the American Diet

*I*n these high-stress times, turning back to the nutritional goodness of whole foods is now being scientifically shown to have the power to drastically improve our health, both physically and mentally. Almost daily, discoveries are made about the specific health benefits of food. Discovering the power of nutrition knowledge and making informed decisions around food choices give us the ability to dramatically change our health. Even the smallest nutritional improvements can lead to noticeable changes in health, appearance, and energy level. On the heels of scientific advancements in food technology, scientists now understand which components of grains create the physiologic effects necessary for healing and disease prevention.

What's to Come

The following chapters will tell you everything you wanted to know about bread but didn't know to ask. Chapters 1 through 5 take you on a tour of the digestive system and explain how the components of bread can help or hinder the intricate processes of digestion and which bread ingredients meet your specific dietary needs. Chapters 6 through 14 contain general bread recipes with guidelines on how to make your own variations. These chapters also give recipes for individuals with various health conditions. As you get into the nitty-gritty of baking, you will find the glossary helpful as well as the list of mail order companies that carry some of those important bread ingredients you may not be able to find.

Whole Foods

The value of macronutrients—fats, carbohydrates, and proteins—in the daily diet depends on their appropriate quantity and quality. The nation's top health organizations agree that we need to minimize our fat intake, reduce our consumption of high-protein animal foods, and eat more foods rich in complex carbohydrates. Whole foods such as whole grains and legumes are plant foods that are high in fiber and consist primarily of complex carbohydrates: exactly what the doctor ordered!

Whole foods are defined as those that are processed as minimally as possible. This results in foods that are in their natural form, exactly as nature intended. They retain not only all of their natural vitamins, minerals, and fiber but also all of the protective substances that science has yet to identify. Whole wheat flour, for example, is more nutritious because the vitamin-containing germ and the fibrous bran are intact, whereas refined white flour has lost all of its insoluble fiber and many vitamins, minerals, and other nutrients in the extensive milling process.

The New Food Pyramid

Whole grains are our key to maintaining health and preventing disease. Grains were once just one of the four basic food groups

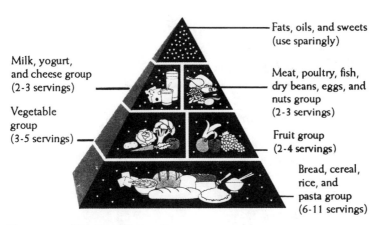

Figure 1.   The Food Pyramid

but are now recognized as the base of the food pyramid and should constitute a majority of our diet. (See Figure 1.) The new food pyramid, released in 1992 by the United States Department of Agriculture, advises Americans to eat six to eleven servings of breads, cereals, and grains each day for weight control, heart health, reduced risk of cancer, and overall nutritional balance. In fact, replacing fat calories with carbohydrate calories has become a national priority. The average fat content in one slice of whole grain bread is around one gram. Each slice of whole grain bread brings you one serving closer to satisfying that daily requirement.

The New FDA Food Label

We are now on the verge of the most extensive overhaul of the nation's health policy, and the U.S. government is taking an active role in trying to reduce health-care costs in the United States through dietary education aimed at disease prevention. The latest tool for nutrition education is the new FDA food label, which supports the FDA's food-labeling regulations. (See Figure 2.) All food manufacturers must comply with these regulations

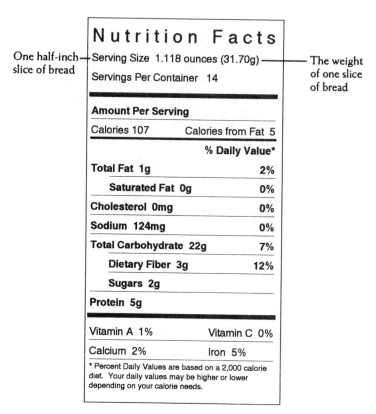

One half-inch slice of bread

Nutrition Facts

Serving Size 1.118 ounces (31.70g)

The weight of one slice of bread

Servings Per Container 14

Amount Per Serving

Calories 107	Calories from Fat 5

	% Daily Value*
Total Fat 1g	2%
Saturated Fat 0g	0%
Cholesterol 0mg	0%
Sodium 124mg	0%
Total Carbohydrate 22g	7%
Dietary Fiber 3g	12%
Sugars 2g	
Protein 5g	

Vitamin A 1%	Vitamin C 0%
Calcium 2%	Iron 5%

* Percent Daily Values are based on a 2,000 calorie diet. Your daily values may be higher or lower depending on your calorie needs.

Figure 2. The New FDA Food Label

by using these labels on all commercially produced food products by May 8, 1994. The new food labels include nutritional facts such as calories, protein, and fat as a percentage of recommended daily intake; total fat; and content of vitamin A, vitamin C, calcium, and iron.

Vitamins and Minerals

Vitamins and minerals play essential roles in our body's biochemical processes. Vitamin A, for example, plays an intimate role in vision, cell integrity, hormonal activity, and maintenance of cell nerve sheaths; assists immune reactions; and plays a major role in the manufacture of red blood cells. Vitamin C protects the cells; helps in collagen, bone, and skin formation; and aids in neutralizing the effects of stress on the body. This vitamin is also involved in hormone and amino acid metabolism. Calcium plays a well-known role in bone formation and maintenance, aids in blood clotting, and is involved in enzyme activity, blood pressure maintenance, and regulation of muscle tone. Iron is vital in cellular respiration—the process by which cells generate energy—and every living cell contains iron. These are just a few of the nutrients we need on a daily basis. Pondering the role of these few nutrients clearly defines how the foods we choose affect our well-being.

Bread and Weight Loss

People who are still holding on to the old myth that bread is fattening can now take comfort in finding that just the opposite is true! Bread's high-fiber, complex-carbohydrate content makes it one of the more filling and least fattening foods around. A slice of whole grain bread contains only one gram of fat—less than 10 percent of its calories. Therefore, as long as we avoid high-fat spreads and ingredients, bread can actually be an aid to weight loss. It's true! A 1990 study at the Institute of Aerobics Research in Dallas, Texas, found that the inclusion of eight slices of whole grain bread per day improved carbohydrate, fat, iron, fiber, and calcium intake in the study group while they lost weight.

In two separate research studies with overweight college students bread was found actually to aid in weight loss. In one study, volunteers lost an average of nine pounds over a ten-week period when fed eight slices of whole grain bread a day and given free choice of other foods. In a similar study, one group of volunteers lost an average of fourteen pounds by eating twelve slices of white bread a day, while the second group of volunteers lost an average of nineteen pounds when fed the same amount of high-fiber whole grain bread. The college students lost weight because the generous daily allowance displaced fattier, high-calorie foods from their diet.

Fiber is an additional help in weight loss as it attracts water, is more filling, binds with fats, and helps maintain a clean and motile digestive tract. This book focuses on the health benefits of eating fiber-rich whole grain breads. Nutritionists agree that people rarely get fat from eating carbohydrates; they get fat from eating too much fat! In other words—pass the bread but hold the butter.

The Future of Home Baking with Automatic Bread Makers

The automatic bread maker has been called the Cuisinart of the 1990s. Baking homemade bread has become a routine for hundreds of thousands of Americans. In an age when we understand how vital it is to nurture our bodies and minds, bread has become a satisfying retreat into a healthful, guilt-free habit. Bread machines provide us with the opportunity to have complete control over the quality of our bread ingredients, for example, by allowing us the freedom to choose unrefined vegetable oils instead of the hydrogenated oils found in many store-bought breads. This simple home appliance has given thousands of people who have special dietary restrictions the first opportunity to enjoy palatable and delicious wheat-free, gluten-free, or low-sodium breads.

CHAPTER 2

The Anatomy of Digestion

Good health depends upon not only good food but also good digestion and absorption. Without good digestion and absorption, the health-giving nutrients of bread cannot be optimally used by the body. Therefore, before we can begin to appreciate the nutritive qualities of bread, we must first appreciate and understand the organs of the body that are involved with digestion and the process of digestion itself. (See Figure 3.)

The Organs of Digestion

The alimentary canal is a coiled tube about thirty feet long that passes through the center of the body. It extends from the mouth to the anus and includes the mouth, esophagus, stomach, small intestine, and large intestine or colon. The alimentary canal, together with its accessory organs, the liver, gallbladder, and pancreas, make up the digestive tract. The purpose of the digestive tract is to perform chemical and mechanical digestion, absorption, waste storage, and excretion.

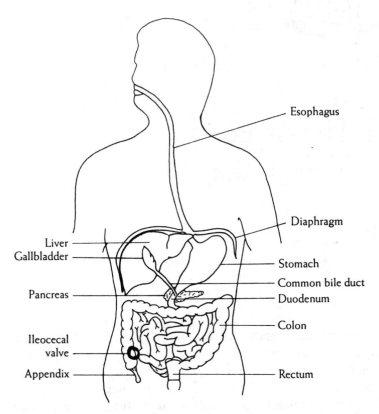

Figure 3. Organs of Digestion

The Process of Digestion

Digestion is a series of physical and chemical changes by which food taken into the body undergoes hydrolysis (addition of water) and is broken down in preparation for absorption from the digestive tract into the bloodstream. Digestion takes place in the alimentary canal. In the upper section of the tract, mechanical digestion is accomplished by the chewing and grinding of food into smaller pieces, which are then pushed along the digestive tract. At appropriate times the food is mixed with digestive juices that cause chemical changes that break down the food into smaller absorbable compounds. At the lower end of the canal, waste products are stored and periodically eliminated from the body.

Why does the aroma of baking bread make my mouth water?

When the brain perceives food, it signals the digestive system that food is on its way. The smell, taste, and sometimes even the thought of food trigger the three pairs of salivary glands to produce saliva. These glands are located under the tongue (sublingual), under the jaw (submandibular), and in front of the ear (parotid). Saliva acts as a wetting agent. It moistens and lubricates food, making it easier to swallow. The average person secretes up to three pints of saliva a day.

How does food move through the digestive tract?

Muscle power, not gravity, moves the food through the alimentary canal. The walls of this tube contain two layers of muscles. One set, the circular muscle layer, encircles the tube, while the other, the longitudinal layer, runs lengthwise along the tube. When food is swallowed, the muscles are stimulated, causing *peristalsis*, waves of muscle contractions. Peristaltic waves quickly move the food to the stomach. These waves continue until the esophagus is emptied of food.

Does most digestion take place in the stomach?

Although we tend to think of the stomach as the center of digestion, very little chemical digestion actually takes place there. Instead, the stomach functions as an internal blender, mechanically processing food so that the nutrients can be extracted. This process is called *mechanical digestion*. The stomach churns food, mixing it with gastric juices to form a milky-colored material called *chyme*. Every thirty seconds or so, peristaltic waves squirt a few milliliters of chyme into the small intestine.

How long does it take for the stomach to empty after a meal?

The stomach takes from two to four hours to empty, depending upon how much is eaten and what is in the meal. Meals that are rich in fiber take longer to leave the stomach than meals that are full of fiber-depleted refined foods. High-fiber meals are said to "delay gastric emptying." This quality is especially important for individuals who suffer from diabetes and hypoglycemia because it slows the rate at which glucose is absorbed from a meal, thereby regulating insulin release and preventing sudden dips in blood glucose levels.

What is gastric juice?

Gastric juice is a highly acidic mixture of hydrochloric acid, enzymes, and mucus that begins chemical digestion and sterilizes the stomach. It is secreted by glands located in the middle portion of the stomach that secrete an average of 2,000 to 2,500 ml of gastric juice a day. The major digestive enzymes found in gastric juice are rennin, which curdles the milk protein casein; pepsin, which begins the process of protein digestion; and lipase, which hydrolyzes fats to form free fatty acids. Gastric juice also contains intrinsic factor, a compound necessary if vitamin B-12 is to be absorbed in the intestine.

Where is food digested?

Although some digestion begins in the stomach, most digestion and absorption take place in the small intestine. The purpose of the small intestine is to finish digestion and absorb nutrients. Since the nutrients freed by digestion are absorbed through the lining of the intestine, the greater the intestinal area, the greater the amount of nutrients absorbed. The lining of the intestine has its surface area greatly increased by an ingenious system of folds, villi, and microvilli. The lining of the small intestine is arranged in folds covered with fingerlike projections called villi. The villi in turn are covered with microvilli, sometimes referred to as the *brush border*. Most of the digestive enzymes found in the small intestine are located on this brush border. These enzymes finish the process of digestion. The freed nutrients then pass through the walls of the villi and into their networks of fine capillaries, veins, and arteries, which lead to the bloodstream and the liver.

How large is the small intestine?

The small intestine is one inch in diameter and lies coiled in the abdominal cavity. The intestinal coil would be approximately twenty feet long if unwound. However, this size is deceptively small, because the folds, villi, and microvilli increase the surface area of the intestine to 250 square meters, roughly the size of a tennis court. Since nutrients can be absorbed only through the intestinal lining, the larger the surface area, the more nutrients that are absorbed.

What is the duodenum?

The first ten inches of the small intestine curve into a backward C shape. This is the duodenum. Every thirty seconds peristaltic waves in the stomach squirt a small amount of chyme into the duodenum. When the duodenum detects the presence of the acidic chyme, it release sodium bicarbonate to neutralize it. This is necessary because the intestinal enzymes will not work in an acid environment. When the duodenum detects the presence of fat in the chyme, it releases bile, which is produced in the liver and stored in the gallbladder. Bile acts as a detergent, forming *micelles* which surround the fat, making it temporarily water soluble. As the micelles approach the brush border, the fats are released to pass through the cell membrane and are absorbed. The pancreas also releases enzymes that split carbohydrates, proteins, and the bile-emulsified fats. Most digestion is completed in the duodenum. The remainder of the small intestine, the *jejunum* and *ileum*, are concerned with absorption.

What happens in the jejunum and ileum?

After the duodenum, the small intestine abruptly turns forward and downward and becomes the jejunum. This is where the final stages of digestion occur and where absorption is completed. Within thirty minutes after chyme has reached the small intestine, most nutrient absorption is completed. Peristaltic waves move the chyme toward the *iliocecal valve* at the end of the small intestine at a rate of one centimeter per minute. The entire journey of a meal through the small intestine takes from three to ten hours.

What is the function of the large intestine?

The large intestine is chiefly responsible for water and electrolyte absorption, waste storage, and excretion. The colon is about two and one-half inches in diameter with a length of five to six feet. This makes the large intestine wider in diameter but much shorter in length than the small intestine. As fecal material moves through the colon, water is absorbed, and the feces become progressively drier. About 95 percent of the water and sodium entering the colon each day is absorbed. The last eight inches of the colon is called the rectum, which ends with the anal canal. Defecation occurs via the anus.

What other function does the colon have?

The colon also serves as a garden for bacteria, and over four hundred bacterial species live there. The most common bacteria include *Bacteriodes, Bifidobacterium, Fusobacterium, Clostridium, Eubacterium, Peptococcus,* and *Peptostreptococcus.* Some of these bacteria help the body by secreting vitamin K, which is important for proper blood clotting. Dietary fiber is a major food source for these microorganisms. They are able to digest much of the soluble fiber that reaches the colon and then ferment the break-down products into chemicals called short-chain fatty acids (SCFAs). These compounds are then absorbed into the bloodstream and travel to the liver and other body organs. These fermentation products may protect against cancer and heart disease and be useful in the treatment of diabetes and obesity.

How is the liver involved in digestion?

The liver is the largest gland in the body and one of the most important organs. Nutrient-rich blood leaving the intestines must first pass through the liver. Here poisonous substances either formed in the colon or eaten in food are detoxified. Liver cells also remove from the blood and store excess amounts of iron and vitamins A, B-12, and D and secrete the bile used to emulsify fats. Bile is stored in a pear-shaped organ called the gallbladder until it is needed. Then the gallbladder contracts, and bile is squirted into the duodenum.

What is the pancreas?

The pancreas is a grayish-pink gland that secretes the digestive enzymes that are released into the duodenum. It is also the organ that secretes insulin, one of the hormones most important for carbohydrate metabolism. Individuals with Type I diabetes have lost the ability to secrete insulin.

Where does digestion take place?

Digestion takes place whenever and wherever food comes into contact with digestive enzymes. Salivary glands at the base of the tongue secrete enzymes that begin the digestion of carbohydrates. Enzymes secreted by the lining of the stomach are involved in protein, fat, and milk digestion. Enzymes secreted by the pancreas are squirted into the duodenum, where fat, protein, and carbohydrate digestion continues. The last site of digestion occurs on the brush border of the small intestine, where the last of the fat, protein, and carbohydrate digestion occurs. There are no digestive enzymes in the colon. All digestion and most absorption are completed by the time food leaves the small intestine.

What are enzymes?

Enzymes are a special kind of protein that speed up (catalyze) biological reactions that otherwise would occur very slowly. Digestive enzymes are enzymes that break down larger molecules of food into smaller molecules that can be absorbed by the body. They are named by adding the suffix "ase" to the substrate they digest. Amylases (amyl=starch) break down complex carbohydrates (starches) into their component sugars, proteases break down protein into amino acids, and lipases break down lipids into fatty acids.

CHAPTER 3

Bread, Fiber, and Prevention

*B*read is one of those rare foods that not only fills the stomach but also stimulates the senses, satisfies the appetite, and nourishes the body, and it is able to accomplish all of this with a minimum of calories and very little fat. Because of this, bread (and other grain products) are getting a lot more respect these days. The U.S. Department of Agriculture has recently promoted the bread and cereal group from being just one of the four basic food groups to forming the entire base of the new food pyramid. This means that breads and grains are no longer just part of a healthy diet; they are now the foundation upon which a healthy diet is built. This may seem like a lot to expect from a little grain, but breads and cereals have worked hard to earn their new reputation.

Bread and Nutrition

Nutrition experts and government health agencies recommend that we consume a diet high in complex carbohydrates and fiber and low in fat and animal protein. Whole grain bread fits this profile perfectly. Bread is an excellent source of complex carbohydrate, a time-release source of energy. Bread is also a good source of low-fat protein. Depending upon the ingredients, bread can be cholesterol- and saturated-fat-free and even fat-free. However, bread's most important claim to fame is its fiber content.

Bread and Fiber

Grandma called fiber "roughage" and likened it to a broom that kept the colon swept clean and tidy. She recommended it for constipation. It wasn't until the mid-1960s that fiber attracted the attention of the scientific community. That was when T. L. Cleave, a surgeon in the Royal Navy, hypothesized that a wide range of diseases might be due to the amount of unnatural, refined carbohydrates in the modern diet. Building upon this observation, Denis Burkitt and Hugh Trowell, English physicians working in Uganda, noticed that diseases of the colon were rare among the natives, who consumed a high-fiber, high-carbohydrate diet. Burkitt and Trowell hypothesized that the fiber in some way protected against the development of colorectal cancer. Today, as the result of extensive investigations, researchers have a whole new view of what fiber is and what it does. Instead of being viewed as an inert broom, fiber is now considered to be a very active component of the diet.

How nutritious is bread?

Bread is low in fat and high in complex carbohydrates (starch). Adding bread to any meal will help to balance out its fat content and bring it into compliance with the 15 percent protein, 30 percent fat, and 55 percent carbohydrate profile that most government and health agencies recommend. Whole grain bread is just what the doctor ordered as an addition to today's highly refined food-on-the-run-type diet. Bread is also a source of calcium and iron, two minerals that Americans often lack in their diet, as well as vitamin E, vitamin B-1, and folacin.

My child is a poor eater, but he likes bread. How can I increase the protein and caloric content of his bread?

Bread can be an excellent source of protein and calories needed for growth during childhood. The addition of legume flours such as garbanzo flour and soy flour will increase both the quantity and quality of the protein in bread, as will the addition of milk, yogurt, soymilk, and eggs. Heart-healthy calories can be added by including canola, high-oleic safflower, or olive oil; nuts; seeds; and legume or nut butters to the bread recipes.

How can I increase the iron content of bread?

Iron-rich ingredients that can be added to bread include dried prunes and prune juice, raisins, blackstrap molasses, wheat bran and germ, sunflower seeds, almonds, walnuts, and dates. However, some of these foods also contain phytic acid, which may reduce the amount of iron available for absorption. Since vitamin C counteracts this effect of phytic acid, it is wise to make a habit of including a source of vitamin C with each meal that contains bread. Vitamin C–rich spreads for bread can be found in Chapter 6.

Is bread fattening?

In a word, no. Current research strongly suggests that it is the fat, not the calories, in foods that causes weight gain. A diet high in complex carbohydrate like those found in bread is associated with weight (fat) loss. Whole grain breads also contain significant amounts of fiber, which also aids the weight watcher in feeling satisfied.

What is dietary fiber?

Dietary fiber is a general term, and there is no one accepted definition. Hugh Trowell in 1976 defined fiber as "remnants of plant cells resistant to hydrolysis by the alimentary enzymes of man. It is composed of cellulose, hemicelluloses, oligosaccha-rides, pectins, gums, waxes and lignin." Later he expanded that definition to include all indigestible plant materials, not just those found in the cell wall.

Some researchers feel that this definition is also too limiting and that dietary fiber should include all organic and inorganic matter found in plant cells that resists chemical digestion by human digestive enzymes. Some researchers also believe the definition perhaps should include all edible fiber that is indigest-ible, such as chitin from fungi and crustaceans and fiberlike compounds from animals as well as partially synthetic materials.

How many types of dietary fiber are there?

Since each source of dietary fiber has its own unique chemical and physical properties, there are as many kinds of fiber as there are sources. However, most types of dietary fiber have the following characteristics in common:

- They are either soluble (able to dissolve) or insoluble in the watery chyme.
- They are either are viscous (gel-forming in the chyme) or nonviscous.
- They are easily fermented by bacteria in the colon or resist complete fermentation (nonfermentable).
- Their effects are limited to the gastrointestinal tract, or they can affect the entire body.

Based on these properties, dietary fiber can be divided into two main categories:

1. fiber that is soluble, viscous, fermentable, and affects the entire body

2. fiber that is insoluble, nonviscous, nonfermentable, and affects only the gastrointestinal tract.

It is important to remember that these classifications are for
convenience only and that some types of fiber may actually
possess characteristics of both types. Figure 4 shows the loca-
tions of soluble and insoluble fiber in grain kernels.

What effect does insoluble/nonviscous/nonfermentable fiber have on the gastrointestinal tract?

Fibers in this category resist digestion by the bacteria of the
colon and for the most part exit the colon in the same form in
which they are eaten. These fibers appear to affect only the
gastrointestinal tract. They work by increasing the mass of the
feces, increasing the frequency of bowel movements, reducing
the amount of time food takes to travel through the intestine, and
decreasing the pressure within the colon.

Which cereals contain insoluble/nonviscous/ nonfermentable fiber?

Whole wheat, wheat bran, wheat germ, brown rice, rice bran,
and rice polish are good sources of insoluble fiber.

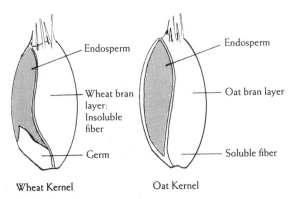

Wheat Kernel   Oat Kernel

Figure 4.   Grain Kernels Showing Location of Soluble and Insoluble
Fiber.

What effect does soluble/viscous/fermentable fiber have on the gastrointestinal tract?

This kind of fiber enters the large intestine or colon in the same form in which it was eaten. However once in the colon, it is partially or completely broken down by the colonic bacteria into carbohydrates and their derivatives, which are then fermented by the bacteria to gases (carbon dioxide, hydrogen, and methane), lactic acid, and short-chain fatty acids (SCFAs; mainly acetate, propionate, and butyrate.)

These fermentation products may act locally in the colon by changing the pH of the feces or interacting with the cells of the colon. The SCFAs can also be absorbed into the bloodstream and affect organs all over the body. In particular, SCFAs may affect the liver and influence the metabolism of glucose and fats.

Which breads contain soluble/viscous/fermentable fiber?

All baking products containing oats (oat bran, oat flakes, oak flour), barley (barley flour, barley flakes), legume flours (garbanzo bean flour, soybean flour), and dried or fresh fruits and vegetables (raisins, prunes, apples) are sources of soluble fiber.

What is constipation, and how can fiber help to prevent it?

There is no one correct definition of constipation. Some people think of constipation as the passing of stools that are "too" hard, "too" small, or "difficult" to pass. Others "feel" constipated if they do not have a bowel movement at least once each day. Professional definitions of constipation run from the allopathic view of less than three bowel movements per week to the naturopathophic view of less than three movements per day.

Many people find that increasing the amount of fiber in their diet will eliminate constipation. Both soluble and insoluble fiber have a laxative effect on the colon. Insoluble fiber increases the size of the stool, thereby stimulating the colonic muscle movements and decreasing transit time through the large intestine. Wheat bran is noted for its laxative properties, since it can absorb as much as three times its weight in water. Rice bran may absorb even more. Soluble fiber may also increase the softness and volume of feces by virtue of its water-holding and gas-producing properties.

Remember, lack of sufficient dietary fiber is only one cause of constipation. Other causes include lack of exercise, delaying defecation, prolonged use of laxatives, stress, hypothyroidism, dehydration, and certain drugs, including iron-, calcium-, and aluminum-containing compounds.

What are hemorrhoids?

Hemorrhoids are varicose veins that occur in the anus or rectum. They cause rectal itching, pain, and sometimes red blood in the stools. Many women who have had children are familiar with this problem. Increasing dietary fiber can decrease constipation and straining, which may prevent hemorrhoids in some people and relieve symptoms in those who are already afflicted.

What is irritable bowel syndrome, and how can fiber help?

Irritable bowel syndrome (IBS), or spastic colon, is a gastrointestinal disease that affects gut motility. Sufferers either have diarrhea without abdominal pain or alternating bouts of diarrhea and constipation accompanied by abdominal pain. At the moment there is no one known cause of IBS. Food allergies and intolerances may be responsible for some cases.

Dietary fiber not only works to relieve constipation in IBS patients; it can also alleviate diarrhea. This is because fiber, wheat bran in particular, normalizes gut motility. Wheat bran slows down the overly active colon and speeds up the overly slow. As little as four slices of whole grain bread daily was sufficient to improve symptoms in one group of patients.

How does dietary fiber help to reduce high cholesterol levels?

By now everyone knows that oat bran, a soluble fiber, has been found to decrease cholesterol levels in men who have high blood cholesterol levels. Many theories have been proposed to explain this phenomenon, but so far how soluble fiber accomplishes this feat is largely unknown. Here are some of the major theories.

- SCFAs formed in the colon by the bacterial breakdown of soluble fiber travel to the liver, where they may regulate the production of cholesterol. Two of the SCFAs that may be involved are propionate and acetate.
- Low levels of blood insulin may reduce cholesterol, since high insulin levels seem to increase cholesterol production. Soluble fiber may be able to keep blood insulin levels more uniform because it slows the release of food from the stomach.
- The gelling properties of most soluble fiber makes the reabsorption of cholesterol less efficient, thereby decreasing the amount of cholesterol available.
- Alpha tocotrienol, a component of barley and oats, also may inhibit cholesterol synthesis.

The cholesterol-lowering effects of fiber are probably due to a combination of factors. To receive all the benefits that whole grains have to offer, it is wise to eat a wide variety of grains, not just soluble fiber.

Can fiber protect me from colon cancer?

The evidence that a diet rich in whole grains, particularly wheat bran and cellulose, protects the colon from cancer is convincing. Exactly how that protection is accomplished, however, is a matter of considerable controversy. It may be a direct effect of the fiber diluting potential carcinogens in the colon, the effect of a fermentation by-product, or another compound associated with the fiber. Wheat bran is able to prevent experimentally produced cancer in lab animals.

High-fiber diets have been associated with a decreased risk of not only colon cancer but also breast, prostate, and stomach cancer.

Why is a high-fiber diet important for diabetics?

Most physicians recommend that their diabetic patients follow a low-fat, high-carbohydrate diet. A diet rich in complex carbohydrates increases the sensitivity of non-insulin-dependent diabetics to insulin, and it may also reduce their risk of developing heart disease. Soluble fiber has been shown to slow down the rate at which the stomach empties, thereby reducing the rate at which glucose is absorbed from the digestive tract. This slow release of glucose in turn keeps the blood sugar levels even and reduces the need for insulin. This is particularly important for insulin-dependent diabetics.

What is diverticular disease, and how can a high-fiber diet help?

Diverticula are small pouches that occur in the wall of the colon. These diverticula are likely to occur as individuals age and are referred to as *diverticular disease*. This disease has increased since the turn of the century, when American diets started to become more refined and depleted of fiber. Diverticular disease appears to be rare among nonindustrialized populations.

Symptoms of diverticular disease include intermittent cramping or continuous lower abdominal discomfort, constipation, and feelings of distention. However, only 20 percent of those afflicted with diverticular disease have any symptoms, and the appearance of symptoms seems to be associated with a low-fiber diet. Today, most physicians recommend a high-fiber diet for their diverticular patients. Wheat bran is often the fiber of choice.

Can fiber cause a mineral deficiency?

Some researchers are concerned that the thirty to thirty-five grams of fiber that some health professionals recommend is too high and may cause a mineral imbalance. This fear is based on the fact that the phytic acid present in some fibers may absorb and bind minerals such as zinc, calcium, and iron and make them unavailable to the body. However, this binding of minerals appears to be minimal in the normal mixed diet. Strict vegetarians and Third World populations with high-fiber diets do not show signs of inadequate mineral absorption. It is safe to say that the health risk to Americans lies in the low-fiber diet, not the high-fiber diet.

CHAPTER 4

Bread, Fiber, and Disease

*T*he preceding chapter discussed the role bread and fiber play in the prevention and treatment of disease. In this chapter we will see that bread can have a negative effect on some individuals who cannot tolerate some of its usual ingredients.

Individuals who have adverse reactions to these ingredients find that they cannot benefit from the good properties of bread for fear of reaction to the bad. These reactions usually take two forms. Some individuals have an immune response or allergy to particular ingredients found in bread, and some have an intolerance. In order to benefit from the effects of fiber and other related compounds in breads, such individuals must buy specialty breads, often at high cost. A bread machine can give these individuals back all the sensory delights of eating fresh bread. When you make the bread in your own machine, you have control over all the ingredients that go into it.

What is an allergy?

When the body is under attack by a parasite, bacteria, or virus, the immune system launches a counterattack, designed to stop the intruders and eventually destroy them. In order to be able to do this, the immune system must be able to tell the difference between cells that belong to the body and cells that do not. They do this by reading the proteins on the surface of the cells that they encounter. An allergy is a case of mistaken identity. The immune system misreads the proteins on an innocent cell or protein from a harmless food and launches an attack against it. The familiar symptoms of allergy are a by-product of this attack.

What are the symptoms of food allergy?

The most common symptoms of food allergy include dark circles under the eyes, runny nose, diarrhea, chronic infections, skin rashes and itching, and headaches.

Which bread ingredients are common allergens?

The proteins found in wheat, milk, eggs, and yeast are not tolerated by the immune systems of some people. Fortunately, delicious bread can be made by substituting other ingredients for these foods.

What is a food intolerance?

Food intolerance is a broad classification that includes many types of reactions to foods. These can include lack of specific enzymes to digest lactose, sorbitol, or sucrose; reactions to food additives such as monosodium glutamate (MSG) and sulfites; and reactions to pharmacological agents naturally present in foods such as histamine, tyramine, and methylxanthines. These reactions do not involve the immune system, but often the symptoms are very similar to food allergy symptoms. A very common food intolerance is lactose intolerance. Individuals who are lactose intolerant do not have enough of the enzyme lactase to break down the sugar lactose. Lactose then reaches the colon intact, where it causes bloating, cramps, and diarrhea.

What is the difference between a food allergy and a food intolerance?

A food allergy is the result of an interaction between the immune system and a food protein. Usually the allergic reaction is mild and only causes ill health in the long run. However, some instances of food allergy can be life-threatening. If you suspect that you have a food allergy, be sure to see your physician for advice.

A food intolerance does not involve the immune system and, other than toxic reactions to food additives or toxins, rarely causes immediate life-threatening reactions. Intolerances can, however, lead to malabsorption of food and gradual malnutrition.

What are the treatments for food allergies and food intolerances?

The treatment for either problem is the same: the foods that cause the allergy or intolerance must be eliminated from the diet.

Can't I buy bread in the store that does not contain the ingredients to which I am allergic?

Yes, but always read the labels very carefully, because some ingredients can hide under a variety of names. Unless the bread specifically claims to be free of the substance to which you are sensitive, do not buy it. For example, wheat can hide under a distressing number of names. Breads can be bought that are marked as wheat-free, and these are fine for those individuals who are allergic to wheat. Wheat-free breads, however, are not necessarily gluten-free and cannot be used by celiacs. Celiac patients must buy only bakery products that are labeled as gluten-free.

Home bread making is an important option for individuals with allergies and intolerances because it gives back to these people control over the ingredients in their bread. Freshly baked bread also is more nutritious, tastes better, and is often cheaper to make than buy.

I suffer from food allergies. Is it safe for me to purchase my bread ingredients from bulk containers?

Because the bulk containers in stores often share scoops, cross contamination can easily occur. If you suffer from allergies or intolerances to a food item, it is always safer to purchase that ingredient in a sealed bag or container. This is especially important if you have a severe reaction to minute amounts of the offending food.

I am allergic to cow's milk. Can I make my bread with goat's milk?

If you are allergic to cow's milk, there is a chance you may be able to tolerate goat's milk. However, you should be aware that the proteins found in cow's milk are very similar to the proteins found in goat's milk and that many allergy suffers are sensitive to both. If you are unsure about which foods you should eliminate, be sure to check with your doctor first.

Goat's milk can be purchased at your local health-food store and some supermarkets. If you purchase unpasteurized goat's milk, it must be scalded before being added to the bread machine. Unpasteurized milk contains serum proteins that weaken the gluten structure of the dough.

What is gluten-sensitive enteropathy?

Gluten-sensitive enteropathy is a group of disorders that result from a toxic reaction between certain amino acids found in grains and the lining of the intestine. The gliadin (found in wheat and rye) and the prolamin (found in barley and oats) in some way cause the destruction of the villi of the small intestine, resulting in severe malabsorption.

In *celiac disease* (celiac sprue), this toxic reaction manifests itself with symptoms of malabsorption including chronic iron-deficiency anemia, weight loss, constipation, diarrhea, and abdominal pain. In *dermatitis herpetiformis*, the toxicity is manifested on the skin, causing small, itchy water blisters on areas exposed to pressure. *Transient gluten hypersensitivity* is an extremely rare condition seen primarily in children under the age of two. Unlike celiac disease and dermatitis herpetiformis, which are inherited lifelong conditions, transient gluten hypersensitivity appears to be self-limiting, and eventually children with this problem seem to be able to tolerate gliadin and prolamin normally.

All forms of gluten-sensitive enteropathy are treated by adherence to a gliadin- and prolamin-free diet. This means that no wheat, rye, oats, or barley can be consumed. Avoiding these grains allows the intestinal villi and skin lesions to eventually heal. If you have been diagnosed with this disease, it is strongly recommended that you join one of the support groups listed in Chapter 7. This book is not meant to be a complete guide for celiac disease.

Can individuals with celiac disease eat bread?

Yes, but only breads made from rice flour; vegetable flours such as tapioca, potato, and potato starch flour; and legume flours such as chick-pea and soy flour. Since wheat can hide under many names, buy only ingredients that are labeled as gluten-free. Because these flours lack the gluten necessary to make the bread rise, special directions and ingredients must be used to make a satisfactory loaf. For more information, see Chapter 7.

I have celiac disease and am also lactose intolerant. Can I substitute soymilk?

The inability to digest lactose in celiacs is often temporary and will return when the intestinal lining heals. Until then, soymilk can be substituted for cow's milk. But be sure you read the label. Some soymilks are sweetened with barley malt. Use only fortified soymilks that are either unsweetened or contain brown rice syrup. If in doubt, use the unsweetened kind.

I am on a low-fat diet. Should I make only fat-free breads?

Bread is a naturally low-fat food, and most of the recipes in this book are low-fat, low-cholesterol, and low in saturated fat. Fat-free breads can be made, but a small amount of fat is desirable in bread. It will increase the shelf life of the bread and aid in the absorption of fat-soluble vitamins. The most fattening aspect of bread is the spreads that are put on top of it. For nutritious and delicious ideas for healthy butters and spreads, see Chapter 6.

CHAPTER 5

Bread, Dough, and Bread Machines

*B*read is considered to be one of the simpler pleasures of life: an uncomplicated food in an otherwise complicated world. After all, what could be more easy and natural than the simple melding of wheat, water, and yeast to form bread?

Were it that simple! Anyone who regularly bakes bread knows just how temperamental bread dough can be. This is because dough is not just an inanimate lump of wheat and water. It is alive, and like all living organisms prone to fits of unpredictability. If the temperature or humidity is wrong, your dough may turn fickle and not rise, or if you change brands of flour, your dough may expand with enough abandon to overflow your machine! What was enough water on Monday may be too much on Friday, and so on. Each bread machine also has its own personality and quirks.

The easiest way to avoid problems with bread dough and your bread machine is to make bread frequently and get to know your machine and what a proper bread dough should look like in your machine. For example, if you make gluten-free bread, your dough is going to look substantially different from the dough of a whole wheat bread. Don't be afraid to lift the cover during the mixing and kneading cycle to become familiar with what's going on, and don't be afraid to try unfamiliar flours and new or unusual ingredients. Half the fun of using a bread machine comes from experimenting. Remember, bread baking is not just a cooking exercise; it is a sensory experience. So if you are having a bad bread day, cheer up, and look for the answer to your problem here.

Kitchen Science

What is sourdough?

Sourdough is the result of yeast (*Saccharomyces exiguus*) and its natural activity as these living organisms eat the sugars in grain flours. Sourdough starter is necessary and can be obtained from a local bakery, from a friend's old batch, or from a health-food store; or you can make your own. Mix one cup flour with one cup water and a pinch of yeast. Stir until creamy. Leave the mixture alone for a week in a large glass or plastic container, unrefrigerated. At this point the starter is a living culture and can be kept on hand to make sourdough bread anytime.

What type of yeast works best in bread machines?

Bread machines are designed to use only active dry yeast. Cake yeast is not recommended.

How does yeast make bread rise?

Yeast feeds on the sugar in the bread dough and converts the carbohydrates in the bread into carbon dioxide gas. The air pockets that form in the dough give the finished loaf its airy texture.

What is the difference between bleached wheat flour and unbleached white flour?

The bleaching process used to whiten flour involves chlorination, while unbleached flour is lightened naturally through aging. Chlorine is suspect as a carcinogen, and for this reason the unbleached variety is preferable.

Why is there a separate time setting for whole wheat bread?

The function of the whole wheat setting is to extend the rising time for whole grain breads, which need more time than their white flour counterparts. If your machine does not have a whole wheat cycle, you can unplug the machine after the first knead cycle and restart it.

Is it possible to test baker's yeast that may be old?

Mix one teaspoon of yeast, one-quarter teaspoon of sugar, and one-quarter cup of lukewarm water. If activation does not occur within five to ten minutes the yeast is dead.

What is the function of fat in a recipe?

Butter, margarine, or vegetable or nut oils are added to make bread tender, give a soft crumb, and help to preserve bread. It is possible to replace the fat with fruit juice concentrates, low-fat yogurt, fresh fruit, fruit puree such as apple sauce, or other high-water content foods, which will add moisture while keeping the overall fat content low. High-pectin fruits such as tart apples, blackberries, cherries, cranberries, grapefruit, grapes, lemons, limes, and oranges work best to replace fat. In savory breads, miso, a fermented soybean paste, also works as a fat substitute.

What is the purpose of kneading yeast bread?

Kneading serves as the primary method of mixing the dough once it's too hard to be mixed with a spoon, allowing air to be worked through the dough and furthering the development of gluten.

What is the purpose of adding dehydrated milk to the batter?

Dry or fresh milk can be added to enhance the flavor and increase the nutritional value of bread. Milk solids include protein, lactose (milk sugar), and minerals. One tablespoon per cup of flour is usually the recommendation. In such small amounts the benefits are minimal. Lactose (milk sugar) provides a source of food for the growing yeast. If you cannot tolerate milk products, just use a sugar such as honey or maple sugar as food for the yeast. Milk is not necessary.

Kitchen Techniques

Is it necessary to sift flour?

Sifting is unnecessary, as all commercial flour today is presifted. Sifting could actually result in an inaccurate measurement. Therefore, if you decide to sift your ingredients, sift them together after measuring.

What is the easiest technique for measuring sticky syrups and honey?

When a recipe calls for oil and honey or molasses, measure the oil first and don't rinse the spoon off. The honey or molasses won't stick and will slide off the spoon easily.

What is the best way to store bread?

For consumption within three days, store bread in a plastic bag at room temperature. Refrigeration seems to make bread soggy. Place a piece of celery in the bag to keep it fresher. Freezing works well to preserve flavor and nutritional quality up to three months. To freeze, first let the loaf cool completely, then wrap the whole unsliced bread in a plastic bag, plastic wrap, foil, or freezer paper. Bread can be thawed by wrapping in foil and reheating in a 300-degree oven for twenty minutes.

Once bread has started to dry out, is there any way to salvage it?

Old bread makes great croutons, french toast, bread crumbs for cooking, and a base for bread pudding.

Is it possible to have whole nuts make it through the vigorous mixing cycle if this is the effect you want?

If nuts, raisins, or fruit bits are added at the beginning of the mixing cycle, they will most likely be pulverized and unrecognizable by the end. However, they can be added at the end of the first kneading cycle, and some machines can be programmed to beep at that time to remind you to add them.

Bread Nutrition Knowledge

Can grain flours and bean flours be used interchangeably?

Bean (legume) flours can be used in place of up to 50 percent of grain flours in a recipe. Bean flours, such as garbanzo and soybean, increase the protein content of bread considerably but tend to result in a denser loaf. They work well when used in combination with whole grain flours. One cup of whole wheat flour, for example, can be replaced with one cup of soy flour in a small-loaf recipe.

Is there any danger of food poisoning when eggs are left in the machine with the timer set for baking several hours in advance?

Yes. Do not under any circumstances use the timer setting with perishable ingredients such as eggs, milk, or meat. Even cottage cheese, cream cheese, sour cream, and yogurt should be baked immediately.

What is the nutritional value of whole grain flour?

Whole wheat flour is ideal for the health conscious because it consists primarily of complex carbohydrates with fiber and a little fat. Freshly milled flour contains the highest concentrations of nutrients, and many people find it worth the time and investment to purchase a mill for the home. Another popular option for in-home milling is the flour mill attachment for the Champion juicer, which you may already have. If you choose store-bought flour over milling your own, insist on flour with a "pull date" displayed on the package so you can be assured of freshness. As flour ages, the vitamins in it start to oxidize, resulting in a depreciating nutritional value. Storing flour in the freezer slows the aging process, extending the life span.

Perfect Loaf Troubleshooting

What is wrong when a loaf comes out soggy or sunken?

This indicates too much liquid, which may be hidden in ingredients such as fresh vegetables or fruits. Reduce the amount of liquid in the recipe by one tablespoon or add two tablespoons of flour. Always use a standard liquid measuring cup and spoons and check measurement at eye level. If the bread is actually gummy or doughy, you may need to increase the amount of yeast.

What is wrong when a loaf comes out knotty, with an uneven top that is heavy, coarse, or dry?

This can be caused by inaccurate flour measurement. Always use measuring cups designed for dry measurement. If the dough ball appears to be too dry, add more liquid a tablespoon at a time. If the dough is too moist, adjust by adding more flour one tablespoon at a time.

What causes a mushroom-top-shaped loaf?

A mushroom top results when bread rises too fast and collapses. Reducing the yeast by a quarter teaspoon will usually solve the problem. If you are still getting too much rise in your loaf, then reduce the amount of sweetener used. Sugar feeds the yeast, which makes the bread rise. Reducing the liquid by one to two tablespoons will often result in a more dense loaf. The last resort, which has only a minimal effect on bread's rising, is to increase the salt. Salt inhibits the yeast activity slightly.

What alteration can be made for loaves that are not rising enough?

Add more yeast. Even where a recipe calls for only one teaspoon of yeast, a recipe can benefit from up to four teaspoons, depending on the moisture in the air, the sweetener used, and the age of the yeast. The rule of thumb is one teaspoon of yeast per cup of whole grain flour used. One tablespoon of vital gluten added for each cup of whole grain or low-gluten flour will also increase the rise.

Other solutions include using a longer baking cycle; reducing the amount of salt; increasing the sugar, which feeds the yeast; and increasing the water by a tablespoon or so.

Some machines, such as the Panasonic, are built to have the yeast drop into the dough from a special compartment. However, when using whole grain or low-gluten flours, it is beneficial to sprinkle the yeast directly on top of the dry ingredients.

What causes incomplete cooking on the top of the loaf?

This is caused by exceeding the dough capacity of the machine. Reduce the recipe by 10 to 20 percent or try a recipe for a smaller loaf.

What will prevent dry or crumbling loaves?

Fat or liquid will add moisture to bread recipes. Vegetable oil, water, or fruit juice in small quantities will makes dough smoother and result in a softer loaf. One-half cup of low-fat cottage cheese does wonders for whole grain breads in this respect. Eggs are also a great dough conditioner and binder.

Bread Machine Expert

Will bread mixes work in the bread machines?

Some bread mixes are designed specifically for bread machines. Others, particularly gluten-free mixes, do not work well at all. It is best to stick with mixes that indicate they have been developed for electric bread machines.

Is the order in which the ingredients are added to the baking pan important?

Some machines have specific directions in the owner's manuals to add liquid first, then dry ingredients. This is important for machines that do not have a separate yeast compartment, as the yeast must stay separate from the liquid and sweetener until it is time for it to be activated.

Can the large (two-pound-loaf) machines make small-, medium-, and large-size loafs?

The two-pound-loaf machines are at their best with the large and medium recipes. These are the recipes that call for three to five cups of whole grain flour. The bottom of the bread pan is big enough that the small-size recipes end up very short and flat, which makes for stubby bread slices.

Can the small (one- to one-and-a-half-pound-loaf) machines make small- and medium-size loaves equally as well?

A small or one-pound loaf usually calls for around two and a half cups of whole grain flour. The small loaves work just fine in this size pan. In fact, the wheat-free and low-gluten recipes actually work best as small loaves. For higher gluten breads, use the medium-size recipes, which average around three cups of flour and make a more practical size loaf for sandwich slices and toast.

When should the yeast be added to the dough?

Usually the yeast can be added along with the other ingredients. This is actually preferable when using whole grain flours, because it allows the yeast maximum activation time and therefore more rising action for these low-gluten flours. However, when using the timer function on your machine, it is important to keep the yeast dry until mixing time. Therefore, adding the liquid ingredients first, the dry ingredients second, and the yeast last on top works best. Some machines, such as the Panasonic, have a separate compartment for the yeast to be used with the delayed starting function.

Is it necessary to clean the baking pan after each loaf?

No, just wipe out the flour residue with a paper or cloth towel. Just twisting the paddle around a few times is usually sufficient to knock out any remaining bread bits caught around the base of the paddle. If more vigorous cleaning is needed, just soak the pan in hot soapy water immediately after removing the baked bread. Avoid using any cleaning aids that might scratch the nonstick surface.

CHAPTER 6

Basic Breads

Getting Started

Creating individualized bread recipes is a very rewarding creative process because it results in a deeper understanding of the baking process and allows you the freedom to create many variations of your favorite recipes.

Use the basic bread recipes as a starting place for making your own bread ingredient combinations. Turn to the sections of the book you are particularly interested in to get ideas for the ingredients that are most healthful for you and use them to modify the basic bread recipes to develop your own favorite recipes.

Experimenting is important when using bread machines because there are so many variables involved: the size of your machine, the age of the flours you are using, the temperature of the bread machine when you start the cycle, and the amount of moisture in the air on any given day. By using the basic bread recipes as a base and adding your favorite ingredients, you will find recipes that work best for you and will serve you well as your staple recipes. We have found these simple bread recipes to be consistent and fairly foolproof when used with simple alterations such as adding fruits, nuts, nut butters, herbs and spices or even cheeses and sauces. Experiment with them so you are not limited. Once you have decided on the ingredients you want to use, turn to the section "Perfect Loaf Troubleshooting" in Chapter 5 to help fine-tune your recipe.

It is important for you to know your bread machine. There are many different types on the market. Some machines make extra-large rectangular loaves; others have yeast dispensers, quick bread settings, and whole wheat settings. Some will even make jam!

Bread Crusts

Dress up your bread. Give your loaf a shiny golden crown or a crunchy seeded cap.

For a Glossy Crust

Dissolve ½ teaspoon of cornstarch in ⅓ cup of water; heat the mixture until boiling. Brush top of loaf with mixture and let bake for 10 minutes. Reapply 10 minutes into the bake cycle.

For a Shiny Crust

Brush top of unbaked loaf with 1 egg white mixed with 1 tablespoon water.

For a Golden Crust

Brush top of unbaked loaf with 1 egg yolk. For a golden shine, brush with a whole egg.

For a Tender Crust

Brush loaf with butter or olive oil just before baking or just before you remove it from the machine.

For a Seeded Crust

Brush the top of the unbaked loaf with an egg glaze and sprinkle with ¼ to ½ teaspoon of seeds such as poppyseeds, sesame seeds, psyllium seeds, flaxseeds, or caraway seeds.

For Pebbled Crust

Mix ¼ cup of rolled oats, triticale, rye, barley, or wheat with 2 tablespoons of milk or soymilk. Let sit for ½ hour or until softened and spread on top of unbaked loaf.

Great Bread Spreads

Better Butter

Mix an equal amount of butter and olive oil or canola oil in a blender. Store in refrigerator. The result is a light and refreshing butter substitute that has 50 percent less cholesterol and 50 percent less saturated fat than solid dairy butter.

Instant Apricot Butter

In a blender, combine an equal amount of dried apricots with water. Process until smooth.

Instant Prune Spread

In a blender, combine about ¼ cup apple juice or orange juice with a handful of pitted prunes. This is a wonderful topping for breads, waffles, and pancakes.

Avocado Spread

Lightly mash 1 avocado with 1 big spoonful of salsa for a quick and colorful topping that is the perfect complement to Mexican Corn Bread.

Garlic and Herb Spread

½ pound firm tofu
1 or 2 garlic cloves,
   pressed
2 teaspoons soy sauce

¼ teaspoon dried basil
¼ teaspoon dried oregano
¼ teaspoon dried chives

Blend tofu, garlic, and soy sauce in a blender; place in bowl and stir in the herbs. This delicious sandwich spread is great with thinly sliced raw vegetables on savory breads.

Olivada Spread

2½ tablespoons olive oil
2 garlic cloves, pressed
1½ cups black pitted olives

Pinch each of dried
   oregano, basil, rosemary,
   and thyme

In a blender, blend the olive oil and garlic until smooth and creamy. Add the olives and herbs and blend just until spreadable. This simple olive spread is a quick fix for unexpected guests and has ingredients that are easy to keep on hand. Serve with herbed breads.

Nut Butters

Many nut butters are now available, including peanut, almond, sesame seed, cashew, pistachio, and sunflower. These are simple high-protein spreads that combine well with many whole grain, nutty, or sweet breads. A tablespoon of nut butter on a slice of whole grain bread is a nutritious breakfast for the road.

Tips for Baking Whole Grain Bread

1. To increase the height of a loaf:
   - Use bread flour instead of all-purpose flour; it is higher in gluten.
   - Use the whole grain cycle if your machine has one.
   - If your machine does not have a whole grain cycle, unplug the machine after the first knead and then restart.
   - Add 1 tablespoon of vital gluten (available in your health-food store) for every 1 cup of whole grain flour.
   - Add 1 to 2 teaspoons more yeast.
   - Substitute 1 or more cups of unbleached white flour for an equal amount of whole wheat flour.
2. If you are lactose intolerant or have a milk allergy, substitute soymilk, rice milk, apple juice, goat milk, or almond milk for the cow's milk.
3. If you must reduce sodium or salt, eliminate or reduce the salt and add spices and herbs.
4. Instead of butter or vegetable oil, use heart-friendly olive or canola oil.

Note to the owners of Panasonic/National machines:

- We found that the doughs mixed better if wet ingredients were added first, not last as the instructions recommend.
- When using the yeast dispenser, add an extra teaspoon of yeast to the amount recommended in the recipe.
- Large-size recipes made in the retangular pan had a tendency to lose part of the dough during mixing. This dough falls down around the heating elements and burns while the bread is baking. Our smoke alarm was set off more than once! We recommend that you watch the dough to make sure that it does not climb over the sides of the pan during mixing. The large rectangular loaves of bread that this machine produced were impressive, but they required a few minutes of babysitting.

Basic Wheat Bread

LARGE

1½ cups low-fat milk
2 cups whole wheat bread
  flour
2 cups unbleached bread
  flour

2 tablespoons vital gluten
1 teaspoon salt
2 teaspoons yeast

This is an easy-to-bake beginner's bread that makes a great sandwich. When you have made a few loaves, try some of the variations that follow.

MEDIUM

1⅛ cups low-fat milk
1½ cups whole wheat
  bread flour
1½ cups unbleached bread
  flour

1½ tablespoons vital gluten
¾ teaspoon salt
1½ teaspoons yeast

SMALL

¾ cup low-fat milk
1 cup whole wheat bread
  flour
1 cup unbleached bread
  flour

1 tablespoon vital gluten
½ teaspoon salt
1 teaspoon yeast

Variations for Basic Wheat Bread (Ingredients to Add)

LARGE	MEDIUM	SMALL
Lemon Pepper Bread		
2 teaspoons lemon zest	1½ teaspoons	1 teaspoon
1 teaspoon ground pepper	¾ teaspoon	½ teaspoon
2 tablespoons dried red pepper	1½ tablespoons	1 tablespoon

```
┌─────────────────────────────────────────────────┐
│ Nutrition Facts (based on medium-               │
│ size loaf)                                      │
│ Serving Size 2.439 ounces (69.14g)             │
│ Servings Per Container  10                      │
├─────────────────────────────────────────────────┤
│ Amount Per Serving                              │
│ Calories 147          Calories from Fat 9      │
├─────────────────────────────────────────────────┤
│                       % Daily Value*            │
│ Total Fat 1g                          2%        │
│   Saturated Fat 0g                    0%        │
│ Cholesterol 1mg                       0%        │
│ Sodium 176mg                          0%        │
│ Total Carbohydrate 29g               10%        │
│   Dietary Fiber 2g                    8%        │
│   Sugars 1g                                     │
│ Protein 8g                                      │
├─────────────────────────────────────────────────┤
│ Vitamin A   1%        Vitamin C  0%             │
│ Calcium     4%        Iron      10%             │
├─────────────────────────────────────────────────┤
│ *Percent Daily Values are based on a 2,000     │
│ calorie diet. Your daily values may be higher  │
│ or lower depending on your calorie needs.      │
└─────────────────────────────────────────────────┘
```

LARGE	MEDIUM	SMALL
Garlic Parmesan Bread		
½ cup parmesan cheese	⅓ cup	¼ cup
1 tablespoon garlic powder	2 teaspoons	1½ teaspoons
Crunchy Onion Bread		
½ cup millet seeds	⅓ cup	¼ cup
¼ cup dried onions	3 tablespoons	⅛ cup
Three-Seed Bread		
2 tablespoons flaxseed	1½ tablespoons	1 tablespoon
2 tablespoons psyllium seed	1½ tablespoons	1 tablespoon

LARGE	MEDIUM	SMALL

Three-Seed Bread (continued)

| 2 tablespoons sesame seeds | 1½ tablespoons | 1 tablespoon |

Italian Cheese Nut Bread

| ½ cup pine nuts | ⅓ cup | ¼ cup |
| ½ cup grated romano cheese | ⅓ cup | ¼ cup |

Sunflower Date Bread

½ cup sunflower seeds	⅓ cup	¼ cup
½ cup chopped dates	⅓ cup	¼ cup
¼ cup date sugar	3 tablespoons	⅛ cup

Parsley Caraway Bread

| ½ cup dried parsley | ⅓ cup | ¼ cup |
| 3 tablespoons caraway seeds | 2 tablespoons | 1½ tablespoons |

Spotted Bread

| ⅓ cup millet seeds | ¼ cup | 2½ tablespoons |
| ⅓ cup poppyseeds | ¼ cup | 2½ tablespoons |

Multigrain Bread

LARGE

1½ cups milk
3 cups whole wheat bread flour
1½ cups rolled grain (see variations)

¼ cup seeds (see variations)
3 tablespoons vital gluten
1 teaspoon salt
2½ teaspoons yeast

This is a basic recipe that will allow you to make endless variations. The seeds in this bread make it a real family favorite.

MEDIUM

1⅛ cups milk
2¼ cups whole wheat
   bread flour
1⅛ cups rolled grain (see
   variations)

3 tablespoons seeds (see
   variations)
2 tablespoons vital gluten
¾ teaspoon salt
2 teaspoons yeast

SMALL

¾ cup milk
1½ cups whole wheat
   bread flour
¾ cup rolled grain (see
   variations)

2 tablespoons seeds (see
   variations)
1½ tablespoons vital gluten
½ teaspoon salt
1½ teaspoons yeast

Nutrition Facts (based on medium-size loaf)

Serving Size 2.462 ounces (69.79g)

Servings Per Container   10

Amount Per Serving

Calories 150   Calories from Fat 19

	% Daily Value*
Total Fat 2g	3%
Saturated Fat 0g	0%
Cholesterol 0mg	0%
Sodium 231mg	0%
Total Carbohydrate 27g	9%
Dietary Fiber 2g	8%
Sugars 1g	
Protein 9g	

Vitamin A	1%	Vitamin C	0%
Calcium	5%	Iron	10%

*Percent Daily Values are based on a 2,000 calorie diet. Your daily values may be higher or lower depending on your calorie needs.

Different types of seeds impart different flavors. Here is a list of seeds that work well in bread:

Amaranth
Anise
Caraway
Celery
Fennel
Flaxseed
Millet
Poppyseeds
Psyllium
Quinoa
Sesame
Sunflower

Variations for Multigrain Bread

LARGE	MEDIUM	SMALL
Triticale Sunflower Bread		
1½ cups of rolled triticale	1⅛ cups	¾ cup
¼ cup sunflower seeds	3 tablespoons	2 tablespoons
Oat Rye Bread		
¾ cup rolled oats (not instant)	½ cup	⅓ cup
¾ cup rolled rye	½ cup	⅓ cup
¼ cup caraway seeds	3 tablespoons	2 tablespoons
Barley Quinoa Bread		
1½ cups rolled barley	1⅛ cups	¾ cup
¼ cup quinoa grains	3 tablespoons	2 tablespoons
Multigrain Sunflower Bread		
½ cup rolled oats	⅓ cup	¼ cup
½ cup rolled triticale	⅓ cup	¼ cup

LARGE	MEDIUM	SMALL

Multigrain Sunflower Bread (continued)

LARGE	MEDIUM	SMALL
½ cup rolled barley	⅓ cup	¼ cup
¼ cup sunflower seeds	3 tablespoons	2 tablespoons

Easy Multigrain Bread

1½ cups 5-grain cereal (or 7- or 9-)	1⅛ cups	¾ cup

Muesli Bread

1½ cups muesli	1⅛ cups	¾ cup

Barley Millet Bread

1½ cups rolled barley	1⅛ cups	¾ cup
¼ cup millet seeds	3 tablespoons	2 tablespoons

Oat Flaxseed Bread

1½ cups rolled oats	1⅛ cups	¾ cup
¼ cup flaxseed	3 tablespoons	2 tablespoons

Barley Psyllium Bread

1½ cups rolled barley	1⅛ cups	¾ cup
¼ cup psyllium seeds	3 tablespoons	2 tablespoons

Sesame Oat Bread

1½ cups rolled oats	1⅛ cups	¾ cup
¼ cup sesame seeds	3 tablespoons	2 tablespoons

Fruited Bread

LARGE

1¾ cups milk
2 cups whole wheat bread flour
2 cups unbleached bread flour
2 eggs
¼ cup liquid sweetener

2 tablespoons vital gluten
2 teaspoons seasoning (see variations)
1 teaspoon salt
2½ teaspoons yeast
1 cup dried fruit (see variations)

This recipe is for all who are children or children at heart. It is light and sweet and fun to make. The dried fruit allows you to sneak iron into the diet.

Use the raisin bread cycle if your machine has one. If not, just add the fruit after the first knead. When I'm lazy, I just dump all the ingredients in together and let the fruit be blended into the other ingredients. It smells almost better than it tastes!

MEDIUM

1⅓ cups milk
1½ cups whole wheat
   bread flour
1½ cups unbleached bread
   flour
1 egg and 1 egg white
3 tablespoons liquid
   sweetener

1½ tablespoons vital gluten
1½ teaspoons seasoning
   (see variations)
¾ teaspoon salt
2 teaspoons yeast
¾ cup dried fruit (see
   variations)

SMALL

⅞ cup milk
1 cup whole wheat bread
   flour
1 cup unbleached bread
   flour
1 egg
2 tablespoons liquid
   sweetener

1 tablespoon vital gluten
1 teaspoon seasoning
½ teaspoon salt
1½ teaspoons yeast
½ cup dried fruit

Here are some dried fruits that work well in bread:

Apples	Figs
Apricots	Prunes
Cranberries	Raisins
Currants	Sour cherries
Dates	

Nutrition Facts (based on medium-size loaf)
Serving Size 3.498 ounces (99.16g)
Servings Per Container   10

Amount Per Serving
Calories 210   Calories from Fat 14

	% *Daily Value**
Total Fat 2g	3%
Saturated Fat 0g	0%
Cholesterol 23mg	8%
Sodium 191mg	0%
Total Carbohydrate 43g	14%
Dietary Fiber 2g	8%
Sugars 14g	
Protein 9g	

Vitamin A 3%	Vitamin C 1%
Calcium 5%	Iron 11%

---

*Percent Daily Values are based on a 2,000 calorie diet. Your daily values may be higher or lower depending on your calorie needs.

Variations for Fruited Bread

LARGE	MEDIUM	SMALL
Apricot Bread		
1 cup chopped dried apricots	¾ cup	½ cup
2 teaspoons cinnamon	1½ teaspoons	1 teaspoon
Spiced Apple Bread		
1 cup chopped dried apples	¾ cup	½ cup
2 teaspoons apple pie spice	1½ teaspoons	1 teaspoon

LARGE	MEDIUM	SMALL
Gingered Date Bread		
1 cup chopped dates	¾ cup	½ cup
1 teaspoon powdered ginger	¾ teaspoon	½ teaspoon
Prune Bread		
1 cup chopped prunes	¾ cup	½ cup
2 teaspoons pumpkin pie spice	1½ teaspoons	1 teaspoon
Cranapple Bread		
1 cup dried cranberries	¾ cup	½ cup
Substitute apple juice for milk	Substitute apple juice for milk	Substitute apple juice for milk
Golden Raisin Bread		
1 cup golden raisins	¾ cup	½ cup
1 teaspoon nutmeg	¾ teaspoon	½ teaspoon
1 teaspoon cinnamon	¾ teaspoon	½ teaspoon

Basic Bran Bread

LARGE

1½ cups water
2 tablespoons oil
¼ cup liquid sweetener (see variations)
4 cups whole wheat bread flour

½ cup bran (see variations)
½ cup nonfat milk powder
4 tablespoons vital gluten
1 teaspoon salt
2½ teaspoons yeast

Did your doctor tell you to increase your fiber? This recipe is just what the doctor ordered. Have a few slices for breakfast, and you'll never need worry about regularity again.

MEDIUM

1⅛ cups water
1½ tablespoons oil
3 tablespoons liquid
 sweetener (see
 variations)
3 cups whole wheat bread
 flour

⅓ cup bran (see variations)
⅓ cup nonfat milk powder
3 tablespoons vital gluten
¾ teaspoon salt
2 teaspoons yeast

SMALL

¾ cup water
1 tablespoon oil
2 tablespoons liquid
 sweetener (see
 variations)
2 cups whole wheat bread
 flour

¼ cup bran (see variations)
¼ cup nonfat milk powder
2 tablespoons vital gluten
½ teaspoon salt
1½ teaspoons yeast

These are some sweeteners that work well in bread:

Barley malt syrup
Brown rice syrup
Fruit concentrate
Honey
Molasses

Here are some types of bran that can be added to bread:

Oat bran
Rice bran
Rice polish
Wheat bran
Wheat germ

Nutrition Facts (based on medium-size loaf)

Serving Size 2.802 ounces (79.43g)

Servings Per Container   10

Amount Per Serving

Calories 170   Calories from Fat 26

% *Daily Value**

Total Fat 3g	5%
Saturated Fat 0g	0%
Cholesterol 0mg	0%
Sodium 176mg	0%
Total Carbohydrate 32g	11%
Dietary Fiber 2g	8%
Sugars 6g	
Protein 9g	

Vitamin A	1%	Vitamin C	0%
Calcium	4%	Iron	10%

*Percent Daily Values are based on a 2,000 calorie diet. Your daily values may be higher or lower depending on your calorie needs.

Variations for Basic Bran Bread

LARGE	MEDIUM	SMALL
Honey Wheat Bran Bread		
½ cup wheat bran	⅓ cup	¼ cup
¼ cup honey	3 tablespoons	2 tablespoons
Molasses Wheat Germ Bread		
½ cup wheat germ	⅓ cup	¼ cup
¼ cup blackstrap molasses	3 tablespoons	2 tablespoons
Rice Polish Bread		
½ cup rice polish	⅓ cup	¼ cup
¼ cup brown rice syrup	3 tablespoons	2 tablespoons

Large	Medium	Small
Honey Oat Bran Bread		
½ cup oat bran	⅓ cup	¼ cup
¼ cup honey	3 tablespoons	2 tablespoons
Rice Bran Bread		
½ cup rice bran	⅓ cup	¼ cup
¼ cup barley malt	3 tablespoons	2 tablespoons
Two-Bran Bread		
¼ cup oat bran	3 tablespoons	2 tablespoons
¼ cup wheat bran	3 tablespoons	2 tablespoons
¼ cup molasses	3 tablespoons	2 tablespoons

CHAPTER 7

Gluten-Restricted, and Wheat-, Rye-, Oat-, and Barley-Free Bread

Recommended for: celiac disease, dermatitis herpetiformis, transient gluten sensitivity

Gluten is a complex formed when certain proteins in cereals are kneaded. Gluten has the unique ability to trap the gas generated by the growing yeast, thereby allowing the dough to rise. For example, wheat, which is very high in gluten, produces the highest rising breads; rye, which has less gluten, produces a much denser loaf; and rice, which has no gluten, will not rise at all.

Celiac Disease and Dermatitis Herpetiformis

For the average person, gluten is an excellent protein source. However, individuals who suffer from gluten-induced enteropathy have a toxic reaction to the amino acids gliadin and prolamin in gluten. When the celiac patient eats gluten, these proteins injure the lining of the small intestine by destroying the villi. In a person lacking the absorptive area of the intestinal villi, food is malabsorbed. In those who suffer from dermatitis herpetiformis, gliadin and prolamin cause an inflammatory skin disease with an itchy, blistering rash. Symptoms abate in these diseases only when all traces of gliadin and prolamin are removed from the diet. This eliminates all products containing wheat, rye, oats, and barley and all breads and bakery goods containing gluten.

Baking Gluten-Free Bread

Since only flours containing no gliadin and prolamin can be used to make bread for people with celiac disease or dermatitis herpetiformis, a substitute for gluten must be used to make the dough rise. An excellent substitute for gluten is xanthan gum, a natural product made from *Xanthomonas campestris*. This microorganism is grown in the lab for its cell coat, which is dried and ground to form xanthan gum. Xanthan gum is added as a powder to the dry bread ingredients. One teaspoon is needed for every cup of gluten-free flour. You can buy this product at your local health-food store or order it from the sources listed in the back of the book.

Lactose Intolerance

Some celiac patients also suffer from lactose intolerance. This lactose intolerance is usually temporary, and when the intestinal villi heal, the ability to metabolize lactose reappears. Cereal-free soymilk makes an excellent substitute for milk. Fortified soymilk will also add significant amounts of protein, calcium, vitamin D, and riboflavin to your breads.

Organizations to Contact

For more information on celiac disease or dermatitis herpetiformis, contact one of these organizations:

Canadian Celiac Association
6519–B Mississauga Road
Mississauga, Ontario L5T 1A6
Canada
Phone: (416) 567-7195

Celiac Sprue Association
P.O. Box 31700
Omaha, NE 68131-0700
Phone: (402) 558-0600

Gluten Intolerance Group of North America
P.O. Box 23053, Broadway Station
Seattle, WA 98102-0353
Phone: (206) 325-6980

Tips for Making Gluten-Free Breads

1. Buy a machine that makes the one-and-one-half pound square-type loaf. This will enable you to make medium- and small-size loaves that are easy to slice for sandwiches and toast. Because we do not recommend making large-size gluten-free loaves, this chapter contains only recipes for small and medium loaves.
2. Gluten-free doughs are sticky and difficult to mix. Help your machine by checking on the dough often during the first five to ten minutes. Scrape down the sides of the pan with a soft rubber spatula.
3. Gluten-free dough does not look like ordinary wheat dough. Gluten-free doughs require more liquid and, in some recipes, resemble a batter more than a dough. By observing the dough mixing during the first five to ten minutes, you will get a feel for what gluten-free dough should look like and be able to adjust the liquid and dry ingredients accordingly.

4. The dough will mix more readily if you always add the liquid ingredients first. Do this even if your machine recommends that dry ingredients should go in first.
5. Gluten-free breads require extra yeast to rise. Some recipes will double or triple the amount of yeast called for in a similar recipe made with wheat bread.
6. If your machine has a yeast dispenser, do not use it. The bread will rise higher if you sprinkle the yeast on top of the dry ingredients just before you start the machine.
7. A combination of three or four flours will taste better than a mixture of just one or two flours. The bread will rise higher as well.
8. Never buy your flours from an open bin. They may be contaminated with small amounts of gluten-containing products. Use only products that are sealed in a package.
9. Wheat-free ingredients are not the same as gluten-free products. For more information on how to follow a gluten-free diet, call or write one of the support groups listed earlier in this chapter.
10. Potato starch flour is not the same as potato flour. Potato flour is heavier and does not work well in gluten-free breads.

If you suffer from gluten-sensitive enteropathy, avoid these bread ingredients:

Almond milk sweetened with barley malt
Amaranth*
Barley, barley malt, malt flavoring
Brown rice syrup made with barley malt enzyme
Buckwheat
Distilled white vinegar
Enriched wheat flour
Farina
Flour (unbleached)
Gluten, vital gluten
Graham flour

Millet*
Oat flour, rolled oats, oat bran
Quinoa*
Rye
Semolina
Soymilk sweetened with barley malt or containing pearl barley
Spelt*
Teff*
Triticale
Wheat flour or starch
Wheat germ or bran

*May be suitable, but more information is needed before these grains can be recommended.

Here are some bread ingredients that do not contain gliadin or prolamin:

Arrowroot starch
Baking powder, cereal-free
Corn bran
Corn flour
Corn meal
Corn syrup
Lecithin
Legume flours such as soy flour and garbanzo bean flour
Milk
Nut meals such as almond meal
Nut milks not sweetened with barley malt syrup
Potato, flakes, buds, or flour
Potato starch flour
Rice bran
Rice flour
Rice milk
Rice polish
Rice starch
Soymilks sweetened with brown rice syrup

Tapioca flour
Xanthan gum
Yeast

Sunflower Raisin Bran Bread

Gluten-free, wheat-free, milk-free, lactose-free, high-fiber

MEDIUM

2 cups low-fat fortified,
   plain soymilk
2 cups brown rice flour
⅔ cup rice polish
⅔ cup garbanzo bean flour

⅔ cup potato starch flour
3 tablespoons date sugar
4½ teaspoons xanthan gum
1½ teaspoons salt
5 teaspoons yeast

Use raisin bread cycle and add these at the beep or add after first knead:

1 cup raisins
⅓ cup sunflower seeds

This is a crunchy, sweet bread. The raisins and sunflower seeds make it a good source of iron, and the soymilk and legume flour make it an excellent source of protein.

SMALL

1½ cups low-fat fortified,
   plain soymilk
1½ cups brown rice flour
½ cup rice polish
½ cup garbanzo bean flour

½ cup potato starch flour
2¼ tablespoons date sugar
3 teaspoons xanthan gum
1 teaspoon salt
3 teaspoons yeast

Use raisin bread cycle and add these at the beep or add after first knead:

¾ cup raisins   ¼ cup sunflower seeds

Nutrition Facts (based on medium-size loaf)

Serving Size 4.983 ounces (141.3g)
Servings Per Container   10

Amount Per Serving

Calories 305   Calories from Fat 41

	% Daily Value*
Total Fat 5g	8%
Saturated Fat 1g	5%
Cholesterol 0mg	0%
Sodium 266mg	0%
Total Carbohydrate 63g	21%
Dietary Fiber 3g	12%
Sugars 12g	
Protein 8g	

Vitamin A 0%	Vitamin C 0%
Calcium 4%	Iron 18%

---

*Percent Daily Values are based on a 2,000 calorie diet. Your daily values may be higher or lower depending on your calorie needs.

Yogurt Chive Bread

Gluten-free, wheat-free

MEDIUM

2⅓ cups milk
⅔ cup plain yogurt
2 cups brown rice flour
⅔ cup tapioca flour
⅔ cup potato starch flour
⅔ cup garbanzo bean flour

⅓ cup dried chives
2 tablespoons date sugar
4½ teaspoons xanthan gum
1 teaspoon salt
4½ teaspoons yeast

A nice sandwich bread that goes well with cheese and cold cuts.

SMALL

1¾ cups milk
½ cup plain yogurt
1½ cups brown rice flour
½ cup tapioca flour
½ cup potato starch flour
½ cup garbanzo bean flour

¼ cup dried chives
1½ tablespoons date sugar
3 teaspoons xanthan gum
¾ teaspoon salt
3 teaspoons yeast

Nutrition Facts (based on medium-size loaf)

Serving Size 5.321 ounces (150.8g)
Servings Per Container   10

Amount Per Serving

Calories 249   Calories from Fat 16

% *Daily Value**

Total Fat 2g	3%
Saturated Fat 1g	5%
Cholesterol 3mg	1%
Sodium 261mg	0%
Total Carbohydrate 52g	17%
Dietary Fiber 2g	8%
Sugars 4g	
Protein 7g	

Vitamin A 4%	Vitamin C	2%
Calcium 11%	Iron	8%

*Percent Daily Values are based on a 2,000 calorie diet. Your daily values may be higher or lower depending on your calorie needs.

Brown Rice Bread

Gluten-free, wheat-free, lactose-free, milk-free

MEDIUM

2⅓ cups plain, fortified
    soymilk
2 eggs
2 cups brown rice flour
⅔ cup soy flour
⅔ cup potato starch flour

⅔ cup tapioca flour
½ cup date sugar
4½ teaspoons xanthan gum
1½ teaspoons salt
4½ teaspoons yeast

This makes a nice high loaf that children like. Great for peanut
butter and jelly sandwiches.

Nutrition Facts (based on medium-size loaf)

Serving Size 5.095 ounces (144.4g)

Servings Per Container   10

Amount Per Serving

Calories 255   Calories from Fat 30

	% *Daily Value**
Total Fat 3g	5%
Saturated Fat 1g	5%
Cholesterol 0mg	0%
Sodium 260mg	0%
Total Carbohydrate 54g	18%
Dietary Fiber 2g	8%
Sugars 6g	
Protein 5g	

Vitamin A 11%	Vitamin C 0%	
Calcium 9%	Iron 12%	

---

*Percent Daily Values are based on a 2,000
calorie diet. Your daily values may be higher
or lower depending on your calorie needs.

SMALL

1¾ cups plain, fortified soymilk	½ cup tapioca flour
1 egg and 1 egg white	⅓ cup date sugar
1½ cups brown rice flour	3 teaspoons xanthan gum
½ cup soy flour	1 teaspoon salt
½ cup potato starch flour	3½ teaspoons yeast

Prune Rice Bread

Gluten-free, wheat-free, lactose-free, milk-free, low-fat, high-fiber

MEDIUM

1⅞ cups nonfat fortified, plain soymilk	½ cup rice polish
½ cup nonsweetened applesauce	¼ cup date sugar
2 cups brown rice flour	4½ teaspoons xanthan gum
½ cup garbanzo bean flour	2 tablespoons flaxseeds
	1 teaspoon salt
	4½ teaspoons yeast

Use raisin bread cycle and add these at the beep or add after first knead:

1 cup chopped prunes

This recipe makes a lovely, dark-colored moist loaf. This bread is rich in both soluble and insoluble fiber, and the flaxseeds and prunes are natural laxatives. The soymilk adds protein while making it suitable for celiacs who are temporarily lactose intolerant.

SMALL

1½ cups nonfat fortified, plain soymilk	⅓ cup rice polish
⅓ cup nonsweetened applesauce	3 tablespoons date sugar
	3 teaspoons xanthan gum
1½ cups brown rice flour	1½ tablespoons flaxseeds
⅓ cup garbanzo bean flour	¾ teaspoon salt
	3½ teaspoons yeast

Use raisin bread cycle and add these at the beep or after the first knead:

¾ cup chopped prunes

Nutrition Facts (based on medium-size loaf)
Serving Size 4.906 ounces (139.1g)
Servings Per Container   10

Amount Per Serving
Calories 251   Calories from Fat 27

% *Daily Value**
Total Fat 3g   5%
  Saturated Fat 1g   5%
Cholesterol 21mg   7%
Sodium 271mg   0%
Total Carbohydrate 52g   17%
  Dietary Fiber 4g   16%
  Sugars 10g
Protein 8g

Vitamin A   4%   Vitamin C   1%
Calcium   4%   Iron   15%

*Percent Daily Values are based on a 2,000 calorie diet. Your daily values may be higher or lower depending on your calorie needs.

Rice and Raisin Bread

Gluten-free, wheat-free, milk-free, lactose-free

MEDIUM

2½ cups low-fat cereal-free
    soymilk
2 cups brown rice flour
1 cup white rice flour
1 cup tapioca flour

⅓ cup date sugar
4½ teaspoons xanthan gum
1¼ teaspoons salt
4½ teaspoons yeast

Use raisin bread cycle and add 1 cup raisins (soak overnight in apple juice for best flavor) at the beep or add after first knead.

Nutrition Facts (based on medium-size loaf)

Serving Size 5.431 ounces (154.0g)

Servings Per Container   10

Amount Per Serving

Calories 330   Calories from Fat 22

% *Daily Value**

Total Fat 2g	3%
Saturated Fat 1g	5%
Cholesterol 0mg	0%
Sodium 249mg	0%
Total Carbohydrate 72g	24%
Dietary Fiber 3g	12%
Sugars 13g	
Protein 6g	

Vitamin A 12%		Vitamin C	1%
Calcium	9%	Iron	10%

*Percent Daily Values are based on a 2,000 calorie diet. Your daily values may be higher or lower depending on your calorie needs.

This dense, chewy bread is a great way to start the day. I soak my raisins in ginger juice for an added punch and serve the bread with tea.

SMALL

1⅔ cups low-fat cereal-free soymilk
1½ cups brown rice flour
¾ cup white rice flour
¾ cup tapioca flour

¼ cup date sugar
3 teaspoons xanthan gum
¾ teaspoon salt
3 teaspoons yeast

Use raisin bread cycle and add these at the beep or add after first knead:

¾ cup raisins

Baked Apple Bread

Gluten-free, wheat-free, milk-free, lactose-free

MEDIUM

1⅓ cups cereal-free vanilla soymilk
1 cup nonsweetened applesauce
1⅓ cups tapioca flour
1⅓ cups white rice flour

1⅓ cups brown rice flour
½ cup date sugar
4½ teaspoons xanthan gum
1½ teaspoons salt
1 teaspoon cinnamon
4½ teaspoons dry yeast

Use raisin bread cycle and add these at the beep or add after first knead:

¾ cup diced, peeled apple

This bread is so good it will tempt even those who are not gluten intolerant. It is a high-rising, moist loaf that makes a great breakfast bread. When toasted, it tastes like baked apples.

SMALL

1 cup cereal-free vanilla soymilk	1 cup brown rice flour
¾ cup nonsweetened applesauce	⅓ cup date sugar
1 cup tapioca flour	3½ teaspoons xanthan gum
1 cup white rice flour	1 teaspoon salt
	¾ teaspoon cinnamon
	3½ teaspoons dry yeast

Use raisin bread cycle and add these at the beep or add after first knead:

½ cup diced, peeled apple

Nutrition Facts (based on medium-size loaf)

Serving Size 4.533 ounces (128.5g)

Servings Per Container   10

Amount Per Serving

Calories 229   Calories from Fat 13

	% *Daily Value**
Total Fat 1g	2%
Saturated Fat 0g	0%
Cholesterol 0mg	0%
Sodium 232mg	0%
Total Carbohydrate 51g	17%
Dietary Fiber 2g	8%
Sugars 4g	
Protein 4g	

Vitamin A	6%	Vitamin C	2%
Calcium	5%	Iron	7%

*Percent Daily Values are based on a 2,000 calorie diet. Your daily values may be higher or lower depending on your calorie needs.

Sesame Butter Rice Bread

Gluten-free, wheat-free, lactose-free, milk-free

MEDIUM

2¼ cups cereal-free vanilla
   soymilk
⅓ cup honey
⅓ cup sesame seed butter
   (tahini)
2 cups brown rice flour

1 cup tapioca flour
1 cup potato starch flour
4½ teaspoons xanthan gum
1 teaspoon salt
4½ teaspoons yeast

The oil from the sesame butter gives this loaf a rich taste. Try it with one of the spreads from Chapter 6.

Nutrition Facts (based on medium-size loaf)

Serving Size 5.426 ounces (153.8g)

Servings Per Container   10

Amount Per Serving

Calories 347   Calories from Fat 59

	% Daily Value*
Total Fat 7g	11%
Saturated Fat 1g	5%
Cholesterol 0mg	0%
Sodium 253mg	0%
Total Carbohydrate 67g	22%
Dietary Fiber 2g	8%
Sugars 9g	
Protein 6g	

Vitamin A 11%	Vitamin C 1%
Calcium 9%	Iron 13%

---

*Percent Daily Values are based on a 2,000 calorie diet. Your daily values may be higher or lower depending on your calorie needs.

SMALL

1½ cups cereal-free vanilla
   soymilk
¼ cup honey
¼ cup sesame seed butter
   (tahini)
1½ cups brown rice flour

¾ cup tapioca flour
¾ cup potato starch flour
3 teaspoons xanthan gum
¾ teaspoon salt
3½ teaspoons yeast

Dated Poppyseed Bread

Gluten-free, Wheat-free, Lactose-free

MEDIUM

2¼ cups lactose-free milk
⅓ cup blackstrap molasses
⅓ cup sesame seed butter
   (tahini)
2 cups brown rice flour
1 cup tapioca flour

½ cup potato starch flour
½ cup rice polish
4½ teaspoons xanthan gum
2 tablespoons poppyseeds
1 teaspoon salt
4½ teaspoons yeast

Use raisin bread cycle and add these at the beep or add after
first knead:

½ cup chopped dates

A good snack bread for children. It's rich in iron as well as
flavor.

SMALL

1½ cups lactose-free milk
¼ cup blackstrap molasses
¼ cup sesame seed butter
   (tahini)
1½ cups brown rice flour
¾ cup tapioca flour

⅓ cup potato starch flour
⅓ cup rice polish
3 teaspoons xanthan gum
1½ tablespoons poppyseeds
¾ teaspoon salt
3 teaspoons yeast

Use raisin bread cycle and add these at the beep or add after
first knead:

⅓ cup chopped dates

Nutrition Facts (based on medium-size loaf)
Serving Size 5.567 ounces (157.8g)
Servings Per Container 10

Amount Per Serving

Calories 346   Calories from Fat 67

% *Daily Value**

Total Fat 7g	11%
Saturated Fat 1g	5%
Cholesterol 2mg	1%
Sodium 260mg	0%
Total Carbohydrate 66g	22%
Dietary Fiber 3g	12%
Sugars 13g	
Protein 7g	

Vitamin A	3%	Vitamin C	1%
Calcium	19%	Iron	24%

*Percent Daily Values are based on a 2,000 calorie diet. Your daily values may be higher or lower depending on your calorie needs.

Peanut Butter and Apple Rice Bread

Gluten-free, wheat-free, lactose-free, milk-free

MEDIUM

2¼ cups unsweetened
   apple juice
2 tablespoons honey
⅓ cup natural peanut
   butter
2 cups brown rice flour

1 cup tapioca flour
1 cup potato starch flour
4½ teaspoons xanthan gum
1 teaspoon salt
4½ teaspoons yeast

Use raisin bread cycle and add these at the beep or add after first knead:

½ cup chopped, dried
   apple

A good bread for those who are also lactose intolerant. It is a good protein source.

SMALL

1¾ cups unsweetened
   apple juice
1½ tablespoons honey
¼ cup natural peanut
   butter
1½ cups brown rice flour

¾ cup tapioca flour
¾ cup potato starch flour
3½ teaspoons xanthan gum
¾ teaspoon salt
3½ teaspoons yeast

Nutrition Facts (based on medium-size loaf)

Serving Size 5.390 ounces (152.8g)

Servings Per Container   10

Amount Per Serving

Calories 330   Calories from Fat 47

	% Daily Value*
Total Fat 5g	8%
Saturated Fat 1g	5%
Cholesterol 0mg	0%
Sodium 268mg	0%
Total Carbohydrate 66g	22%
Dietary Fiber 3g	12%
Sugars 4g	
Protein 5g	

Vitamin A 0%	Vitamin C 38%
Calcium 2%	Iron 10%

---

*Percent Daily Values are based on a 2,000 calorie diet. Your daily values may be higher or lower depending on your calorie needs.

Use raisin bread cycle and add these at the beep or add after first knead:

⅓ cup chopped, dried
    apple

Seeded Onion Rice Bread

Gluten-free, wheat-free, lactose-free

MEDIUM

2½ cups lactose-free milk
⅓ cup natural peanut
    butter

⅓ cup sesame seeds
2 tablespoons poppyseeds
2 teaspoons caraway seeds

Nutrition Facts (based on medium-size loaf)

Serving Size 5.527 ounces (156.7g)

Servings Per Container   10

Amount Per Serving

Calories 346   Calories from Fat 81

	% *Daily Value**
Total Fat 9g	14%
Saturated Fat 2g	10%
Cholesterol 3mg	1%
Sodium 294mg	0%
Total Carbohydrate 59g	20%
Dietary Fiber 3g	12%
Sugars 4g	
Protein 9g	

Vitamin A 3%		Vitamin C 2%	
Calcium 16%		Iron 14%	

---

*Percent Daily Values are based on a 2,000 calorie diet. Your daily values may be higher or lower depending on your calorie needs.

2 cups brown rice flour
1 cup tapioca flour
1 cup potato starch flour
4½ teaspoons xanthan gum

2 tablespoons dried onion
flakes
1 teaspoon salt
4½ teaspoons yeast

Serve thin slices of this bread with hot soup. The protein in the peanut butter enhances the protein of the rice.

SMALL

1⅔ cups lactose-free milk
¼ cup natural peanut
butter
1½ cups brown rice flour
¾ cup tapioca flour
¾ cup potato starch flour
3 teaspoons xanthan gum
¼ cup sesame seeds

1½ tablespoons poppyseeds
1½ teaspoons caraway
seeds
1½ tablespoons dried
onion flakes
¾ teaspoon salt
3 teaspoons yeast

Banana Rice Bread

Gluten-free, wheat-free, high-fiber

MEDIUM

1½ cups cereal-free
soymilk
1 cup ripe bananas, mashed
2 eggs
2 cups brown rice
½ cup garbanzo bean flour

½ cup rice polish
¼ cup date sugar
4½ teaspoons xanthan gum
2 tablespoons flaxseeds
1 teaspoon salt
3½ teaspoons yeast

This is a slightly sweet, protein-rich bread. Serve it warm and toasted to children for an afterschool snack, or treat yourself to a slice or two with a cup of herbal tea.

SMALL

⅞ cup cereal-free soymilk
⅔ cup ripe bananas,
 mashed
1 whole egg and 1 egg
 white
1⅓ cups brown rice
⅓ cup garbanzo bean flour

⅓ cup rice polish
2 tablespoons date sugar
3 teaspoons xanthan gum
1½ tablespoons flaxseeds
¾ teaspoon salt
3 teaspoons yeast

Nutrition Facts (based on medium-size loaf)

Serving Size 4.559 ounces (129.2g)
Servings Per Container   10

Amount Per Serving

Calories 224   Calories from Fat 37

	% *Daily Value**
Total Fat 4g	6%
Saturated Fat 1g	5%
Cholesterol 43mg	14%
Sodium 249mg	0%
Total Carbohydrate 42g	14%
Dietary Fiber 3g	12%
Sugars 3g	
Protein 7g	

Vitamin A 9%	Vitamin C 3%
Calcium 6%	Iron 13%

---

*Percent Daily Values are based on a 2,000 calorie diet. Your daily values may be higher or lower depending on your calorie needs.

CHAPTER 8

High-Fiber Breads

Recommended for: treatment of constipation, diabetes, diverticular disease, high cholesterol, hypoglycemia, irritable bowel syndrome, weight maintenance, and for prevention of cancer, heart disease, and hemorrhoids

T here are two types of components in the food that we eat: the kind that is digested by the enzymes of the gastrointestinal tract and kind that resists digestion by those enzymes. This latter group is frequently referred to as dietary fiber. For the most part, dietary fiber travels through the alimentary canal unchanged until it reaches the large intestine or colon. Once it reaches the colon, one of two things can happen to it: the fiber can pass unchanged through the colon, or it can be digested by the numerous species of bacteria that live there.

Insoluble Fiber

Fiber that resists digestion by the bacteria of the colon also has the ability to reduce the time food takes to travel through the intestine, decrease pressure within the colon cavity, increase the mass of the feces, and increase the frequency of bowel movements. This type of fiber affects only the alimentary canal and is commonly referred to as insoluble fiber.

Insoluble fiber is recommended for the treatment of constipation, diverticular disease, irritable bowel syndrome, and hemorrhoids.

Soluble Fiber

Fiber that is digested by the bacteria of the colon is broken down into carbohydrates, which can then be fermented. The fermentation products that result are absorbed into the blood and so can affect many areas of the body, not just the colon.

Fermentable fiber is usually referred to as soluble fiber because of its ability to dissolve in the chyme and form a gel. Soluble fiber has the ability to increase the time food remains in the stomach, increase the volume and softness of the feces, and decrease blood cholesterol levels. It may also regulate appetite, affect the liver, and influence the metabolism of fats and glucose. The fiber found in soybeans may even be able to alleviate some of the symptoms of menopause.

Soluble fiber is recommended for the prevention of cancer, heart disease, and obesity and is useful in the treatment of diabetes, hypoglycemia, high blood cholesterol, and irritable bowel syndrome.

Fiber and Bread

The cereal grains that are commonly used to make bread are naturally rich in both fermentable/soluble and nonfermentable/insoluble types of fiber as well as vitamin E, iron, and calcium. Since each grain and legume flour has its own unique type of fiber, it is best to eat a wide variety of fiber sources in order to obtain all the benefits that this nutrient can offer. Fortunately, with bread variety is not only easy but also delicious.

The bran naturally found in whole grain cereals reduces how high the bread dough will rise. Breads made with whole grain all-purpose flour will be low and dense. A higher, lighter loaf can be obained by using only whole wheat bread flour (which contains more gluten) and by adding vital gluten to the flour. Add one tablespoon of vital gluten for each cup of whole grain flour. Tips on making whole grain breads are in Chapter 6.

Here are some laxative additions to bread:

Apples, apple juice, applesauce
Flaxseed
Prunes, prune juice
Psyllium seed
Rice bran
Wheat bran

Here are some sources of soluble fiber:

Apples, applesauce, unfiltered apple juice
Barley flour, rolled barley
Carrots
Garbanzo bean flour
Rolled oats, oat flour, oat bran

Here are some sources of insoluble fiber:

Brown rice
Nuts
Rice bran
Rice polish
Seeds
Wheat bran
Wheat germ
Whole wheat

Psyllium Seed Bran Bread

High-fiber, lactose-free, milk-free, low-fat

LARGE

1½ cups low-fat vanilla
  soymilk
½ cup applesauce
4 cups whole wheat bread
  flour
½ cup wheat bran

4 tablespoons gluten
4 tablespoons psyllium
  seeds
1 teaspoon salt
2 teaspoons yeast

This is a wonder laxative bread. Have a few slices toasted in the morning.

Nutrition Facts (based on medium-size loaf)

Serving Size 2.664 ounces (75.53g)
Servings Per Container   10

Amount Per Serving

Calories 146   Calories from Fat 7

	% *Daily Value**
Total Fat 1g	2%
Saturated Fat 0g	0%
Cholesterol 0mg	0%
Sodium 186mg	0%
Total Carbohydrate 31g	10%
Dietary Fiber 2g	8%
Sugars 0g	
Protein 9g	

Vitamin A 0%	Vitamin C 1%
Calcium 2%	Iron 10%

*Percent Daily Values are based on a 2,000 calorie diet. Your daily values may be higher or lower depending on your calorie needs.

MEDIUM

1 1/8 cups low-fat vanilla
   soymilk
1/3 cup applesauce
3 cups whole wheat bread
   flour
1/3 cup wheat bran

3 tablespoons gluten
3 tablespoons psyllium
   seeds
3/4 teaspoon salt
1 1/2 teaspoons yeast

SMALL

3/4 cup low-fat vanilla
   soymilk
1/4 cup applesauce
2 cups whole wheat bread
   flour
1/4 cup wheat bran

2 tablespoons gluten
2 tablespoons psyllium
   seeds
1/2 teaspoon salt
1 teaspoon yeast

Whole Wheat and Crunchy Millet Bread

High-fiber, milk-free, lactose-free

LARGE

2 cups soymilk
1 cup tofu
2 tablespoons olive oil
2 tablespoons fruit juice
   concentrate
4 cups whole wheat bread
   flour

1/2 cup garbanzo bean flour
2/3 cup millet
2/3 cup sunflower seeds
1 teaspoon salt
4 teaspoons yeast

This wholesome garbanzo and wheat flour bread has a delightful texture from the addition of crunchy millet and the chewy sunflower seeds.

MEDIUM

1½ cups soymilk
¾ cup tofu
1½ tablespoons olive oil
1½ tablespoons fruit juice
   concentrate
3 cups whole wheat bread
   flour

⅜ cup garbanzo bean flour
½ cup millet
½ cup sunflower seeds
¾ teaspoon salt
3 teaspoons yeast

SMALL

1 cup soymilk
½ cup tofu

2 cups whole wheat bread
   flour

Nutrition Facts (based on medium-size loaf)

Serving Size 4.255 ounces (120.6g)
Servings Per Container   10

Amount Per Serving

| Calories 275 | Calories from Fat 77 |

	% *Daily Value**
Total Fat 9g	14%
Saturated Fat 1g	5%
Cholesterol 0mg	0%
Sodium 182mg	0%
Total Carbohydrate 41g	14%
Dietary Fiber 4g	16%
Sugars 3g	
Protein 12g	

Vitamin A	7%	Vitamin C	0%
Calcium	8%	Iron	19%

*Percent Daily Values are based on a 2,000 calorie diet. Your daily values may be higher or lower depending on your calorie needs.

1 tablespoon olive oil
1 tablespoon fruit juice
  concentrate
⅓ cup millet

¼ cup garbanzo bean flour
⅓ cup sunflower seeds
½ teaspoon salt
2 teaspoons yeast

Grain Seed Bread

High-fiber, high-protein

LARGE

2 cups water
2 tablespoons safflower oil
2 tablespoons barley malt
  sweetener
2 cups whole wheat bread
  flour
2 cups millet flour
½ cup oat flour

¼ cup millet seed
¼ cup flaxseed
½ cup soy nuts
2 tablespoons nonfat dry
  milk powder
¾ teaspoon salt
6 teaspoons yeast

One slice of this bread offers one-third of the total recommended fiber for an entire day.

MEDIUM

1½ cups water
1½ tablespoons safflower
  oil
1½ tablespoons barley malt
  sweetener
1½ cups whole wheat
  bread flour
1½ cups millet flour

⅜ cup oat flour
3 tablespoons millet seed
3 tablespoons flaxseed
⅜ cup soy nuts
1½ tablespoons nonfat dry
  milk powder
½ teaspoon salt
4½ teaspoons yeast

SMALL

1 cup water
1 tablespoon safflower oil
1 tablespoon barley malt
   sweetener
1 cup whole wheat bread
   flour
1 cup millet flour
¼ cup oat flour

2 tablespoons millet seed
2 tablespoons flaxseed
¼ cup soy nuts
1 tablespoon nonfat dry
   milk powder
¼ + teaspoon salt
3 teaspoons yeast

Nutrition Facts (based on medium-size loaf)

Serving Size 3.706 ounces (105.1g)
Servings Per Container   10

Amount Per Serving

Calories 258   Calories from Fat 46

	% *Daily Value**
Total Fat 5g	8%
Saturated Fat 1g	5%
Cholesterol 0mg	0%
Sodium 121mg	0%
Total Carbohydrate 45g	15%
Dietary Fiber 7g	28%
Sugars 0g	
Protein 10g	

Vitamin A 0%	Vitamin C 0%
Calcium 2%	Iron 12%

---

*Percent Daily Values are based on a 2,000 calorie diet. Your daily values may be higher or lower depending on your calorie needs.

Three-Grain Bread

High-fiber, high-protein

LARGE

1⅓ cups water
2½ tablespoons canola or
  safflower oil
¼ cup barley malt syrup
¼ cup molasses
⅔ teaspoon salt
1⅓ teaspoons cinnamon

2½ cups whole wheat
  bread flour
⅔ cup barley flour
1 cup millet seed
2 tablespoons nonfat dry
  milk
2½ teaspoons yeast

This high-fiber bread is rich in iron and rich in flavor.

Nutrition Facts (based on medium-size loaf)
Serving Size 2.859 ounces (81.06g)
Servings Per Container   10

Amount Per Serving
Calories 201   Calories from Fat 34

		% Daily Value*
Total Fat 4g		6%
Saturated Fat 0g		0%
Cholesterol 0mg		0%
Sodium 121mg		0%
Total Carbohydrate 37g		12%
Dietary Fiber 4g		16%
Sugars 0g		
Protein 6g		

Vitamin A	0%	Vitamin C	0%
Calcium	6%	Iron	14%

*Percent Daily Values are based on a 2,000 calorie diet. Your daily values may be higher or lower depending on your calorie needs.

MEDIUM

1 cup water
2 tablespoons canola or
    safflower oil
3 tablespoons barley malt
    syrup
3 tablespoons molasses
½ teaspoon salt
1 teaspoon cinnamon

1⅞ cups whole wheat
    bread flour
½ cup barley flour
¾ cup millet seed
1½ tablespoons nonfat dry
    milk
1½ teaspoons yeast

SMALL

⅔ cup water
1¼ tablespoons canola or
    safflower oil
2 tablespoons barley malt
    syrup
2 tablespoons molasses
⅓ teaspoon salt
⅔ teaspoon cinnamon

1¼ cups whole wheat
    bread flour
⅓ cup barley flour
½ cup millet seed
1 tablespoon nonfat dry
    milk
1 teaspoon yeast

Cottage Cheese and Apricot Bread

High-protein, high-fiber

LARGE

⅔ cup water
2 cups low-fat cottage
    cheese
2 tablespoons canola oil
2 tablespoons honey
1 cup dried/chopped
    apricots

5 cups whole wheat bread
    flour
1 teaspoon salt
4 teaspoons yeast

This sweet loaf is moist and chewy as well as a great source of fiber. This will become a favorite recipe for entertaining.

Alone or with a fruit spread, this is an interesting breakfast or tea-time bread.

MEDIUM

½ cup water
1½ cups low-fat cottage
  cheese
1½ tablespoons canola oil
1½ tablespoons honey
¾ cup dried/chopped
  apricots

3¾ cups whole wheat
  bread flour
¾ teaspoon salt
3 teaspoons yeast

Nutrition Facts (based on medium-size loaf)
Serving Size 3.783 ounces (107.2g)
Servings Per Container   10

Amount Per Serving
Calories 227   Calories from Fat 30

                              % *Daily Value**
Total Fat 3g   5%
  Saturated Fat 1g   5%
Cholesterol 2mg   1%
Sodium 301mg   0%
Total Carbohydrate 41g   14%
  Dietary Fiber 3g   12%
  Sugars 5g
Protein 12g

Vitamin A   7%   Vitamin C   0%
Calcium   3%   Iron   12%

*Percent Daily Values are based on a 2,000 calorie diet. Your daily values may be higher or lower depending on your calorie needs.

SMALL

⅓ cup water
1 cup low-fat cottage
  cheese
1 tablespoon canola oil
1 tablespoon honey
½ cup dried/chopped
  apricots

2½ cups whole wheat
  bread flour
½ teaspoon salt
2 teaspoons yeast

Three Bran Bread

High-fiber, low-fat

LARGE

1½ cups nonfat milk
⅓ cup molasses
4 cups whole wheat bread
  flour
¼ cup oat bran

¼ cup rice bran
4 tablespoons vital gluten
1 teaspoon salt
2½ teaspoons yeast

If your machine has a raisin bread cycle, add these when it beeps; if not, add after first knead:

½ cup chopped dates

A dense, rich, chewy bread. Makes wonderful low-fat cheese sandwiches. Or serve it warm with a bit of Better Butter (see Chapter 6 for recipe) spread on the top.

MEDIUM

1⅛ cups nonfat milk
¼ cup molasses
3 cups whole wheat bread
  flour
3 tablespoons oat bran

3 tablespoons rice bran
3 tablespoons vital gluten
¾ teaspoon salt
2 teaspoons yeast

If your machine has a raisin bread cycle, add these when it beeps; if not, add after first knead:

⅓ cup chopped dates

SMALL

¾ cup nonfat milk
2 tablespoons blackstrap molasses
2 cups whole wheat bread flour

2 tablespoons oat bran
2 tablespoons rice bran
2 tablespoons vital gluten
½ teaspoon salt
1½ teaspoons yeast

If your machine has a raisin bread cycle, add these when it beeps; if not, add after first knead:

¼ cup chopped dates

Nutrition Facts (based on medium-size loaf)
Serving Size 2.995 ounces (84.90g)
Servings Per Container   10

Amount Per Serving
Calories 174   Calories from Fat 11

	% *Daily Value**
Total Fat 1g	2%
Saturated Fat 0g	0%
Cholesterol 0mg	0%
Sodium 184mg	0%
Total Carbohydrate 37g	12%
Dietary Fiber 3g	12%
Sugars 7g	
Protein 10g	

Vitamin A 1%	Vitamin C 0%
Calcium 10%	Iron 18%

*Percent Daily Values are based on a 2,000 calorie diet. Your daily values may be higher or lower depending on your calorie needs.

Honey Seed Bread

High-fiber, milk-free, lactose-free

LARGE

1¾ cups water
4 tablespoons olive oil
2 tablespoons honey
4 cups whole wheat bread
   flour
1 cup rolled oats

½ cup rice polish
½ cup flaxseed
4 tablespoons toasted
   (unsalted) sesame seeds
1 teaspoon salt
4 teaspoons yeast

This nutty grain bread is a versatile sandwich bread and great with savory or sweet spreads.

Nutrition Facts (based on medium-size loaf)
Serving Size 3.375 ounces (95.68g)
Servings Per Container   10

Amount Per Serving

Calories 245   Calories from Fat 80

	% Daily Value*
Total Fat 9g	14%
Saturated Fat 1g	5%
Cholesterol 0mg	0%
Sodium 167mg	0%
Total Carbohydrate 37g	12%
Dietary Fiber 4g	16%
Sugars 3g	
Protein 9g	

Vitamin A 0%	Vitamin C 0%
Calcium 5%	Iron 19%

---

*Percent Daily Values are based on a 2,000 calorie diet. Your daily values may be higher or lower depending on your calorie needs.

MEDIUM

1⅓ cups water	⅜ cup rice polish
3 tablespoons olive oil	⅜ cup flaxseed
1½ tablespoons honey	3 tablespoons toasted
3 cups whole wheat bread	(unsalted) sesame seeds
flour	¾ teaspoon salt
¾ cup rolled oats	3 teaspoons yeast

SMALL

⅞ cup water	¼ cup rice polish
2 tablespoons olive oil	¼ cup flaxseed
1 tablespoon honey	2 tablespoons toasted
2 cups whole wheat bread	(unsalted) sesame seeds
flour	½ teaspoon salt
½ cup rolled oats	2 teaspoons yeast

Crunchy Herb Bread

Milk-free, lactose-free, high-fiber

LARGE

1⅓ cups plain soymilk	½ cup millet seeds
2 eggs	4 tablespoons vital gluten
2 tablespoons honey	3 tablespoons Italian
3 cups whole wheat bread	seasoning
flour	1 teaspoon salt
1 cup millet flour	2½ teaspoons yeast

This a wonderfully crunchy bread that fills the air with the subtle scent of Italian seasonings when baked. This attractive millet-studded loaf owes its crunch to the millet seeds.

MEDIUM

1 cup plain soymilk
1 egg plus 1 egg white
1½ tablespoons honey
2¼ cups whole wheat
    bread flour
¾ cup millet flour

⅓ cup millet seeds
3 tablespoons vital gluten
2¼ tablespoons Italian
    seasoning
¾ teaspoon salt
2 teaspoons yeast

SMALL

⅔ cup plain soymilk
1 egg
1 tablespoon honey
1½ cups whole wheat
    bread flour
½ cup millet flour

¼ cup millet seeds
2 tablespoons vital gluten
1½ tablespoons Italian
    seasoning
½ teaspoon salt
1½ teaspoons yeast

Nutrition Facts (based on medium-size loaf)
Serving Size 3.443 ounces (97.61g)
Servings Per Container   10

Amount Per Serving
Calories 236   Calories from Fat 24

	% *Daily Value**
Total Fat 3g	5%
Saturated Fat 1g	5%
Cholesterol 21mg	7%
Sodium 187mg	0%
Total Carbohydrate 45g	15%
Dietary Fiber 5g	20%
Sugars 0g	
Protein 12g	

Vitamin A	6%	Vitamin C	0%
Calcium	4%	Iron	13%

*Percent Daily Values are based on a 2,000 calorie diet. Your daily values may be higher or lower depending on your calorie needs.

Low-Lactose Whole Wheat Bread

High-fiber, lactose-free, high-protein

LARGE

2 cups soymilk or lactose-
   free milk
2 tablespoons olive oil
2 tablespoons molasses
4 cups whole wheat bread
   flour

1 cup millet seeds
1 teaspoon salt
3 teaspoons yeast

This is a low-rising loaf that is perfect for individuals who are lactose intolerant. The molasses adds moisture and depth to this bread.

Nutrition Facts (based on medium-size loaf)

Serving Size 3.307 ounces (93.77g)

Servings Per Container   10

Amount Per Serving

Calories 224   Calories from Fat 37

	% *Daily Value**
Total Fat 4g	6%
Saturated Fat 1g	5%
Cholesterol 0mg	0%
Sodium 182mg	0%
Total Carbohydrate 40g	13%
Dietary Fiber 4g	16%
Sugars 1g	
Protein 8g	

Vitamin A	7%	Vitamin C	0%
Calcium	7%	Iron	14%

*Percent Daily Values are based on a 2,000 calorie diet. Your daily values may be higher or lower depending on your calorie needs.

MEDIUM

1½ cups soymilk or
  lactose-free milk
1½ tablespoons olive oil
1½ tablespoons molasses
3 cups whole wheat bread
  flour

¾ cup millet seeds
¾ teaspoon salt
2 teaspoons yeast

SMALL

1 cup soymilk or lactose-
  free milk
1 tablespoon olive oil
1 tablespoon molasses
2 cups whole wheat bread
  flour

½ cup millet seeds
½ teaspoon salt
1½ teaspoons yeast

Baked Potato with Sour Cream and Chives Bread

High-fiber, high-protein

LARGE

1½ cups nonfat or low-fat
  sour cream
1 egg and 1 egg white
2 tablespoons honey
3 cups whole wheat bread
  flour

⅔ cup potato flakes/buds
¼ cup millet seeds
3 tablespoons vital gluten
1 teaspoon salt
3 teaspoons yeast

If your machine has a raisin bread cycle, add these when it beeps; if not, add after first knead:

3 tablespoons dried chives

MEDIUM

1⅛ cups nonfat or low-fat sour cream
1 egg
1½ tablespoons honey
2¼ cups whole wheat bread flour

½ cup potato flakes/buds
3 tablespoons millet seeds
2½ tablespoons vital gluten
¾ teaspoon salt
2½ teaspoons yeast

If your machine has a raisin bread cycle, add these when it beeps; if not, add after first knead:

2 tablespoons dried chives

Nutrition Facts (based on medium-size loaf)

Serving Size 2.755 ounces (78.11g)

Servings Per Container   10

Amount Per Serving

Calories 201   Calories from Fat 51

	% *Daily Value**
Total Fat 6g	9%
Saturated Fat 4g	20%
Cholesterol 21mg	7%
Sodium 199mg	0%
Total Carbohydrate 32g	11%
Dietary Fiber 2g	8%
Sugars 3g	
Protein 9g	

Vitamin A	1%	Vitamin C	3%
Calcium	4%	Iron	16%

*Percent Daily Values are based on a 2,000 calorie diet. Your daily values may be higher or lower depending on your calorie needs.

SMALL

¾ cup nonfat or low-fat
  sour cream
1 egg white
1 tablespoon honey
1½ cups whole wheat
  bread flour

⅓ cup potato flakes/buds
2 tablespoons millet seeds
2 tablespoons vital gluten
½ teaspoon salt
1½ teaspoons yeast

If your machine has a raisin bread cycle, add these when it
beeps; if not, add after first knead:

1½ tablespoons dried
  chives

CHAPTER 9

High-Protein Breads

Recommended for: children, adolescents, and pregnant or lactating women

Proteins are the building blocks of all living organisms. They are essential to every part of the human cell. In adults, dietary protein is necessary to replace worn-out parts of cells and for maintenance. In the growing child or adolescent, protein is necessary for growth of new body tissues, especially muscle tissue and blood.

Protein and Bread

The protein found in bread is low in saturated fat and cholesterol. This is just the kind of protein that the U.S. Department of Agriculture's new food pyramid recommends that Americans eat. However, most of the protein in bread is obtained from the cereal flours it contains, and these cereal proteins are low in some of the essential amino acids. To increase the quality of the grain protein, a source of legume, nut, seed, or animal protein should be added to the bread or eaten with the bread.

Here are some ingredients that increase the protein quality of bread:

Almonds, almond butter
Amaranth
Bean flakes, dried
Buttermilk
Cashew butter
Eggs, egg whites
Garbanzo bean flour
Milk, dry milk
Peanut butter
Protein powder
Pumpkin seeds
Quinoa
Sesame seeds, sesame butter (tahini)
Soy flour
Soymilk
Soy nuts
Sunflower seeds
Walnuts
Yogurt
All other seeds and nuts

Here are some ingredients that increase the amount of iron in bread:

Apricot butter
Blackstrap molasses
Dates
Prunes, prune juice
Raisins

Breakfast in Bread

High-protein, high-fiber

LARGE

1¾ cups water	4 tablespoons vital gluten
3 cups whole wheat bread flour	4 tablespoons brown sugar
	1 teaspoon salt
1½ cups thick rolled oats	3 teaspoons yeast
¾ cup nonfat instant milk	

If your machine has a raisin bread cycle, add these at the beep; otherwise, add at end of the first knead:

1 cup raisins	⅓ cup sunflower seeds

This is the nutritional equivalent of hot oatmeal with brown sugar and raisins on top. Set your timer and wake up to a very healthy fast-food breakfast. It is sweet and chewy with a stick-to-your-ribs quality.

MEDIUM

1¼ cups water	3 tablespoons vital gluten
2¼ cups whole wheat bread flour	3 tablespoons brown sugar
	¾ teaspoon salt
1⅛ cups thick rolled oats	2 teaspoons yeast
½ cup nonfat instant milk	

If your machine has a raisin bread cycle, add these at the beep; otherwise, add at end of the first knead:

¾ cup raisins	¼ cup sunflower seeds

SMALL

⅞ cup water	2 tablespoons vital gluten
1½ cups whole wheat bread flour	2 tablespoons brown sugar
	½ teaspoon salt
¾ cup thick rolled oats	1½ teaspoons yeast
⅓ cup nonfat instant milk	

If your machine has a raisin bread cycle, add these at the beep; otherwise, add at end of the first knead:

½ cup raisins
3 tablespoons sunflower
   seeds

Nutrition Facts (based on medium-size loaf)

Serving Size 2.269 ounces (64.34g)
Servings Per Container   10

Amount Per Serving

Calories 216   Calories from Fat 32

                              % *Daily Value**

Total Fat 4g   6%
   Saturated Fat 0g   0%
Cholesterol 1mg   0%
Sodium 193mg   0%
Total Carbohydrate 40g   13%
   Dietary Fiber 3g   12%
   Sugars 10g
Protein 11g

Vitamin A   4%   Vitamin C   1%
Calcium   9%   Iron   12%

---

*Percent Daily Values are based on a 2,000 calorie diet. Your daily values may be higher or lower depending on your calorie needs.

Seeded Wheat Bread

High-protein, high-fiber

LARGE

1½ cups water
2 tablespoons safflower oil
4 cups whole wheat bread
   flour
¼ cup nonfat dry milk
¼ cup sunflower seeds

¼ cup sesame seeds
2 tablespoons flaxseeds
2 teaspoons date sugar
⅔ teaspoon salt
4 teaspoons yeast

These fiber-rich grains and seeds team up for a high-texture, nutritious whole grain bread.

Nutrition Facts (based on medium-size loaf)
Serving Size 2.792 ounces (79.14g)
Servings Per Container   10

Amount Per Serving

Calories 191	Calories from Fat 58

	% Daily Value*
Total Fat 6g	9%
Saturated Fat 1g	5%
Cholesterol 0mg	0%
Sodium 119mg	0%
Total Carbohydrate 28g	9%
Dietary Fiber 3g	12%
Sugars 0g	
Protein 10g	

Vitamin A	1%	Vitamin C	0%
Calcium	6%	Iron	14%

*Percent Daily Values are based on a 2,000 calorie diet. Your daily values may be higher or lower depending on your calorie needs.

MEDIUM

1⅛ cups water
1½ tablespoons safflower
    oil
3 cups whole wheat bread
    flour
3 tablespoons nonfat dry
    milk

3 tablespoons sunflower
    seeds
3 tablespoons sesame seeds
1½ tablespoons flaxseeds
1½ teaspoons date sugar
½ teaspoon salt
3 teaspoons yeast

SMALL

¾ cup water
1 tablespoon safflower oil
2 cups whole wheat bread
    flour
2 tablespoons nonfat dry
    milk
2 tablespoons sunflower
    seeds

2 tablespoons sesame seeds
1 tablespoon flaxseeds
1 teaspoon date sugar
⅓ teaspoon salt
2 teaspoons yeast

Cinnamon Raisin Bread

High protein, high-fiber

LARGE

2 cups cottage cheese
1 cup water
½ cup honey
¼ cup vegetable oil
3 teaspoons vanilla extract
5 cups whole wheat bread
    flour

1 teaspoon cinnamon
½ teaspoon allspice
½ teaspoon nutmeg
1 teaspoon salt
4 teaspoons yeast

If your machine has a raisin bread cycle, add these at the beep;
otherwise, add after first knead:

1 cup raisins

This spicy cheese bread makes a hearty breakfast toast.

MEDIUM

1½ cups cottage cheese
¾ cup water
⅓ cup honey
2 tablespoons vegetable oil
2 teaspoons vanilla extract
3¾ cups whole wheat
   bread flour

¾ teaspoon cinnamon
⅓ teaspoon allspice
⅓ teaspoon nutmeg
¾ teaspoon salt
3 teaspoons yeast

If your machine has a raisin bread cycle, add these at the beep; otherwise, add after first knead:

¾ cup raisins

Nutrition Facts (based on medium-size loaf)
Serving Size 4.0322 ounces (114.0g)
Servings Per Container   10

Amount Per Serving
Calories 239   Calories from Fat 37

                        % *Daily Value**
Total Fat 4g   6%
   Saturated Fat 1g   5%
Cholesterol 2mg   1%
Sodium 301mg   0%
Total Carbohydrate 42g   14%
   Dietary Fiber 3g   12%
   Sugars 9g
Protein 12g

Vitamin A   0%   Vitamin C   0%
Calcium   4%   Iron   11%

---

*Percent Daily Values are based on a 2,000 calorie diet. Your daily values may be higher or lower depending on your calorie needs.

SMALL

1 cup cottage cheese
½ cup water
¼ cup honey
2 tablespoons vegetable
    oil
1½ teaspoons vanilla
    extract

2½ cups whole wheat
    bread flour
½ teaspoon cinnamon
¼ teaspoon allspice
¼ teaspoon nutmeg
½ teaspoon salt
2 teaspoons yeast

If your machine has a raisin bread cycle, add ½ cup raisins at the beep; otherwise, add after first knead.

Crunchy Soy Bread

High-protein, high-fiber, lactose-free, milk-free

LARGE

1½ cups vanilla soymilk
2 eggs
4 cups whole wheat bread
    flour
1 cup soy nuts

⅓ cup date sugar
4 tablespoons vital gluten
1 teaspoon salt
2½ teaspoons yeast

MEDIUM

1⅛ cups vanilla soymilk
1 egg and 1 egg white
3 cups whole wheat bread
    flour
¾ cup soy nuts

¼ cup date sugar
3 tablespoons vital gluten
¾ teaspoon salt
1½ teaspoons yeast

SMALL

¾ cup vanilla soymilk
1 egg
2 cups whole wheat bread
    flour
½ cup soy nuts

3 tablespoons date sugar
2 tablespoons vital gluten
½ teaspoon salt
1 teaspoon yeast

```
┌─────────────────────────────────────────────┐
│ Nutrition Facts (based on medium-             │
│ size loaf)                                    │
│ Serving Size 3.115 ounces (88.30g)            │
│ Servings Per Container   10                    │
├─────────────────────────────────────────────┤
│ Amount Per Serving                            │
│ Calories 195          Calories from Fat 34    │
├─────────────────────────────────────────────┤
│                         % Daily Value*        │
│ Total Fat 4g                        6%        │
│   Saturated Fat 1g                  5%        │
│ Cholesterol 21mg                    7%        │
│ Sodium 188mg                        0%        │
│ Total Carbohydrate 33g             11%        │
│   Dietary Fiber 3g                 12%        │
│   Sugars 3g                                   │
│ Protein 13g                                   │
├─────────────────────────────────────────────┤
│ Vitamin A   6%        Vitamin C   0%          │
│ Calcium     6%        Iron       12%          │
├─────────────────────────────────────────────┤
│ *Percent Daily Values are based on a 2,000    │
│ calorie diet. Your daily values may be higher │
│ or lower depending on your calorie needs.     │
└─────────────────────────────────────────────┘
```

Almond Butter Bread

High-protein, high-fiber

LARGE

1¾ cups low-fat milk
¼ cup almond butter
3⅓ cups whole wheat
    bread flour
⅔ cup garbanzo bean flour

4 tablespoons sesame seeds
4 tablespoons vital gluten
¼ cup date sugar
1 teaspoon salt
2½ teaspoons yeast

The almond butter, sesame seeds, and garbanzo bean flour increase the protein quality of this bread. Serve it sliced thinly with soups for a complete and nutritious lunch.

MEDIUM

1⅓ cups low-fat milk
3 tablespoons almond
    butter
2½ cups whole wheat
    bread flour
½ cup garbanzo bean flour

3 tablespoons sesame seeds
3 tablespoons vital gluten
3 tablespoons date sugar
¾ teaspoon salt
2 teaspoons yeast

Nutrition Facts (based on medium-size loaf)

Serving Size 2.992 ounces (84.83g)
Servings Per Container   10

Amount Per Serving

Calories 183   Calories from Fat 48

% *Daily Value**

Total Fat 5g	8%
Saturated Fat 1g	5%
Cholesterol 1mg	0%
Sodium 180mg	0%
Total Carbohydrate 29g	10%
Dietary Fiber 3g	12%
Sugars 4g	
Protein 10g	

Vitamin A 2%	Vitamin C	0%
Calcium 9%	Iron	11%

---

*Percent Daily Values are based on a 2,000 calorie diet. Your daily values may be higher or lower depending on your calorie needs.

SMALL

⅞ cup low-fat milk	2 tablespoons sesame seeds
2 tablespoons almond butter	2 tablespoons vital gluten
1⅔ cups whole wheat bread flour	2 tablespoons date sugar
	½ teaspoon salt
⅓ cup garbanzo bean flour	1½ teaspoons yeast

Dated Almond Butter Bread

High-protein, high-fiber, milk-free, lactose-free

LARGE

1¾ cups vanilla soymilk	½ cup garbanzo bean flour
3 tablespoons almond extract	¼ cup date sugar
¼ cup almond butter	4 tablespoons vital gluten
3½ cups whole wheat bread flour	1 teaspoon salt
	2½ teaspoons yeast
	¾ cup chopped dates

This is a rich, dense bread, high in protein and rich in flavor. Bake it on your whole wheat cycle to increase loaf size. If your machine does not have a whole wheat cycle, restart your machine after the first rise.

MEDIUM

1¼ cups vanilla soymilk	⅓ cup garbanzo bean flour
2 tablespoons almond extract	3 tablespoons date sugar
3 tablespoons almond butter	3 tablespoons vital gluten
2⅔ cups whole wheat bread flour	¾ teaspoon salt
	2 teaspoons yeast
	⅔ cup chopped dates

SMALL

⅞ cup vanilla soymilk
1½ tablespoons almond extract
2 tablespoons almond butter
1¾ cups whole wheat bread flour

¼ cup garbanzo bean flour
⅛ cup date sugar
2 tablespoons vital gluten
½ teaspoon salt
1½ teaspoons yeast
⅓ cup chopped dates

Nutrition Facts (based on medium-size loaf)

Serving Size 3.272 ounces (92.76g)
Servings Per Container   10

Amount Per Serving

Calories 210   Calories from Fat 39

	% *Daily Value**
Total Fat 4g	6%
Saturated Fat 1g	5%
Cholesterol 0mg	0%
Sodium 232mg	0%
Total Carbohydrate 39g	13%
Dietary Fiber 4g	16%
Sugars 10g	
Protein 10g	

Vitamin A 6%	Vitamin C 0%
Calcium 6%	Iron 11%

---

*Percent Daily Values are based on a 2,000 calorie diet. Your daily values may be higher or lower depending on your calorie needs.

Indian Bean Bread

High-protein, milk-free, lactose-free

LARGE

2 cups nonfat soymilk or
  rice milk
2 tablespoons honey
¼ cup safflower oil
2 cups whole wheat bread
  flour
2 cups garbanzo bean flour
½ cup rice polish

4 tablespoons vital gluten
¼ cup flaxseed
2 tablespoons crushed
  coriander seeds
1 teaspoon salt
4 teaspoons yeast
Optional: 1 teaspoon
  mustard seeds or cumin

Almond milk or cow's milk also works well in this recipe. The spices add a subtle flavor, which is accented well with a chutney spread or served with hummus or baba ganouj.

MEDIUM

1½ cups nonfat soymilk or
  rice milk
1½ tablespoons honey
3 tablespoons safflower oil
1½ cups whole wheat
  bread flour
1½ cups garbanzo bean
  flour
⅜ cup rice polish

3 tablespoons vital gluten
3 tablespoons flaxseed
1½ tablespoons crushed
  coriander seeds
¾ teaspoon salt
3 teaspoons yeast
Optional: ¾ teaspoon
  mustard seeds or cumin

SMALL

1 cup nonfat soymilk or
  rice milk
1 tablespoon honey
2 tablespoons safflower oil
1 cup whole wheat bread
  flour
1 cup garbanzo bean flour
¼ cup rice polish

2 tablespoons vital gluten
2 tablespoons flaxseed
1 tablespoon crushed
  coriander seeds
½ teaspoon salt
2 teaspoons yeast
Optional: ½ teaspoon
  mustard seeds or cumin

Nutrition Facts (based on medium-size loaf)
Serving Size 3.301 ounces (93.58g)
Servings Per Container   10

Amount Per Serving

Calories 199   Calories from Fat 60

% *Daily Value**

Total Fat 7g	11%
Saturated Fat 1g	5%
Cholesterol 0mg	0%
Sodium 199mg	0%
Total Carbohydrate 31g	10%
Dietary Fiber 2g	8%
Sugars 3g	
Protein 10g	

Vitamin A	0%	Vitamin C	0%
Calcium	3%	Iron	13%

*Percent Daily Values are based on a 2,000 calorie diet. Your daily values may be higher or lower depending on your calorie needs.

Blueberry Yogurt Bread

High-protein, low-fat

LARGE

2 cups nonfat blueberry
    yogurt
1 cup nonfat milk
2 cups whole wheat bread
    flour
2 cups unbleached bread
    flour

2 tablespoons vital gluten
1 teaspoon salt
2 teaspoons yeast
1 cup drained, frozen
    blueberries

A high-rising, slightly sweet bread with just a hint of berries.

MEDIUM

1½ cups nonfat blueberry
   yogurt
¾ cup nonfat milk
1½ cups whole wheat
   bread flour
1½ cups unbleached bread
   flour

1½ tablespoons vital gluten
¾ teaspoon salt
1½ teaspoons yeast
¾ cup drained, frozen
   blueberries

SMALL

1 cup nonfat blueberry
   yogurt

1 tablespoon vital gluten
½ teaspoon salt

Nutrition Facts (based on medium-size loaf)

Serving Size 3.371 ounces (95.55g)
Servings Per Container   10

Amount Per Serving

Calories 164   Calories from Fat 7

	% *Daily Value**
Total Fat 1g	2%
Saturated Fat 0g	0%
Cholesterol 1mg	0%
Sodium 188mg	0%
Total Carbohydrate 33g	11%
Dietary Fiber 2g	8%
Sugars 3g	
Protein 9g	

Vitamin A 0%	Vitamin C 0%
Calcium 8%	Iron 9%

*Percent Daily Values are based on a 2,000 calorie diet. Your daily values may be higher or lower depending on your calorie needs.

½ cup nonfat milk
1 cup whole wheat bread
 flour
1 cup unbleached bread
 flour

1 teaspoon yeast
½ cup drained, frozen
 blueberries

Cranberry Pumpkin Bread

High-protein, milk-free, lactose-free

LARGE

1⅛ cups vanilla soymilk
¾ cup canned pumpkin
⅓ cup blackstrap molasses
2 eggs
4 cups whole wheat bread
 flour

4 tablespoons vital gluten
2 teaspoons pumpkin pie
 spice
1 teaspoon salt
2½ teaspoons yeast
1 cup dried cranberries

Our favorite recipe. This glorious, high-rising, spicy sweet loaf looks as great as it tastes. The sweetness of the bread contrasts with the slightly sour taste of the cranberries, and the rich brown color of the bread contrasts with the bright red of the cranberries.

MEDIUM

¾ cup vanilla soymilk
½ cup canned pumpkin
¼ cup blackstrap molasses
1 egg plus 1 egg white
3 cups whole wheat bread
 flour

3 tablespoons vital gluten
1½ teaspoons pumpkin pie
 spice
¾ teaspoon salt
2 teaspoons yeast
¾ cup dried cranberries

SMALL

½ cup plus 1 tablespoon
 vanilla soymilk
⅓ cup canned pumpkin
⅕ cup blackstrap molasses

2 tablespoons vital gluten
1 teaspoon pumpkin pie
 spice
½ teaspoon salt

1 egg
2 cups whole wheat bread flour

1½ teaspoons yeast
½ cup dried cranberries

Nutrition Facts (based on medium-size loaf)

Serving Size 3.467 ounces (98.29g)

Servings Per Container 10

Amount Per Serving

Calories 169   Calories from Fat 15

	% *Daily Value**
Total Fat 2g	3%
Saturated Fat 0g	0%
Cholesterol 21mg	7%
Sodium 191mg	0%
Total Carbohydrate 33g	11%
Dietary Fiber 3g	12%
Sugars 3g	
Protein 10g	

Vitamin A 31%	Vitamin C 3%
Calcium 9%	Iron 18%

---

*Percent Daily Values are based on a 2,000 calorie diet. Your daily values may be higher or lower depending on your calorie needs.

Garbanzo Bread

High-protein, milk-free, lactose-free

LARGE

1⅞ cups water
2 tablespoons olive oil
2 tablespoons honey
4 cups whole wheat bread flour

½ cup garbanzo bean flour
½ cup chopped walnuts
4 teaspoons yeast
1 teaspoon salt

This medium-dense bread is loaded with lots of chewy walnuts, which help to increase its protein quality.

MEDIUM

1⅜ cups water
1½ tablespoons olive oil
1½ tablespoons honey
3 cups whole wheat bread
    flour

⅜ cup garbanzo bean flour
⅜ cup chopped walnuts
3 teaspoons yeast
¾ teaspoon salt

Nutrition Facts (based on medium-size loaf)
Serving Size 3.122 ounces (88.51g)
Servings Per Container   10

Amount Per Serving	
Calories 188	Calories from Fat 50

	% *Daily Value**
Total Fat 6g	9%
Saturated Fat 1g	5%
Cholesterol 0mg	0%
Sodium 164mg	0%
Total Carbohydrate 30g	10%
Dietary Fiber 2g	8%
Sugars 3g	
Protein 10g	

Vitamin A	0%	Vitamin C	0%
Calcium	1%	Iron	10%

*Percent Daily Values are based on a 2,000 calorie diet. Your daily values may be higher or lower depending on your calorie needs.

SMALL

1 cup water
1 tablespoon olive oil
1 tablespoon honey
2 cups whole wheat bread
   flour
4 tablespoons garbanzo
   bean flour

4 tablespoons chopped
   walnuts
2 teaspoons yeast
½ teaspoon salt

CHAPTER 10

Lactose-Free Breads

Recommended for: lactose intolerance

*L*actose, or milk sugar, is the main carbohydrate present in milk. It is digested by an enzyme called lactase, which lies on top of the intestinal lining. When lactase is not present or when it is produced in limited quantity, all of the lactose is not digested and absorbed. The undigested lactose is then able to reach the large intestine, where it attracts water into the colon, producing gas, cramps, diarrhea, and bloating.

Lactose Intolerance

Some individuals are unable to digest lactose because they lack sufficient quanities of lactase. In fact, the majority of the world's population lose the ability to digest lactose after weaning. It is estimated that as many as thirty million people in the United States, including two million elementary school children, are lactose intolerant. Some individuals who are lactose intolerant find that they can tolerate small amounts of milk products without developing symptoms. Others find that they must supplement the missing enzyme in order to consume milk products. Lactase can be purchased in stores in the form of a tablet that is swallowed just before consuming a milk product or as a liquid added to milk. Milk can also be purchased that is lactose reduced or lactose-free.

Milk Substitutes

Another alternative for those with lactose intolerance is avoiding milk products altogether. Although milk adds tenderness to the bread texture and increases the protein and calcium content of bread, it is not necessary for bread baking. One of the best substitutes for cow's milk is soymilk. Although regular soymilk is not the nutritional equivalent of cow's milk, fortified soymilk is nutritionally superior to cow's milk. Fruit or vegetable juice is also another easy-to-use alternative. Apple juice works best, but any other juice can be used. If you add an acidic juice such as tomato, pineapple, or citrus, add one teaspoon of baking soda to the ingredients to prevent an acidic flavor to the bread.

If you are lactose intolerant, avoid these ingredients when baking bread:

Any product containing casein, caseinate, sodium caseinate, whey
Butter
Cheese
Cottage cheese
Evaporated milk
Half and half, coffee cream
Heavy cream, whipping cream
Milk (whole, skim, 1 percent, 2 percent, buttermilk, sweet acidophilus)
Nonfat milk solids
Powdered dry milk (whole, nonfat, buttermilk)
Sour cream

Sweetened, condensed milk
Yogurt

Ingredients marked "parve" are milk-free and do not contain lactose. Products containing lactate, lactic acid, and lactalbumin do not contain lactose.

Here are some milk replacements for bread baking:

Fortified soymilk (nonfat, low-fat, or regular)
Fruit juice (fresh or bottled)
Grain beverages such as Rice Dream or Amasake (found in health-food stores)
Lactose-free cow's milk
Lactose-reduced cow's milk
Nut milks such as homemade almond or cashew milk
Vegetable juice (fresh or bottled)

Caraway Apple Bread

Lactose-free, milk-free, high-protein

LARGE

1½ cups apple juice	4 tablespoons caraway
4 tablespoons sesame	seeds
butter (tahini)	3 tablespoons vital gluten
2 cups whole wheat bread	1 teaspoon salt
flour	2½ teaspoons yeast
2 cups unbleached bread	
flour	

A slightly sweet, rich bread with a crispy crust. The apple juice makes this bread light and nutritious.

MEDIUM

1⅛ cups apple juice	3 tablespoons caraway
3 tablespoons sesame	seeds
butter (tahini)	2 tablespoons vital gluten

1½ cups whole wheat
  bread flour
1½ cups unbleached bread
  flour

¾ teaspoon salt
2 teaspoons yeast

SMALL

¾ cup apple juice
2 tablespoons sesame
  butter (tahini)
1 cup whole wheat bread
  flour
1 cup unbleached bread
  flour

2 tablespoons caraway
  seeds
1½ tablespoons vital gluten
½ teaspoon salt
1½ teaspoons yeast

Nutrition Facts (based on medium-size loaf)

Serving Size 2.648 ounces (75.06g)
Servings Per Container   10

Amount Per Serving

Calories 178	Calories from Fat 29

	% *Daily Value**
Total Fat 3g	5%
Saturated Fat 0g	0%
Cholesterol 0mg	0%
Sodium 164mg	0%
Total Carbohydrate 32g	11%
Dietary Fiber 2g	8%
Sugars 0g	
Protein 8g	

Vitamin A 0%	Vitamin C 19%
Calcium 2%	Iron 11%

---

*Percent Daily Values are based on a 2,000
calorie diet. Your daily values may be higher
or lower depending on your calorie needs.

Apple Oat Bread

Lactose-free, milk-free, high-protein

LARGE

1⅞ cups apple juice
2 tablespoons canola oil
3½ cups whole wheat
  bread flour
1 cup oat flour

½ cup oat bran
¼ cup date sugar
4 tablespoons vital gluten
1 teaspoon salt
2½ teaspoons yeast

A wonderful way to start your morning. Make this bread using your timer and wake to the wonderful aroma of the bread. Although it is made with apple juice, this bread is not overly sweet. We like it warm, straight from the machine.

Nutrition Facts (based on medium-size loaf)

Serving Size 3.106 ounces (88.04g)

Servings Per Container   10

Amount Per Serving

Calories 183   Calories from Fat 30

	% Daily Value*
Total Fat 3g	5%
Saturated Fat 0g	0%
Cholesterol 0mg	0%
Sodium 164mg	0%
Total Carbohydrate 35g	12%
Dietary Fiber 3g	12%
Sugars 6g	
Protein 9g	

Vitamin A	0%	Vitamin C	0%
Calcium	1%	Iron	11%

---

*Percent Daily Values are based on a 2,000 calorie diet. Your daily values may be higher or lower depending on your calorie needs.

MEDIUM

1½ cups apple juice
1½ tablespoons canola oil
2⅔ cups whole wheat
 bread flour
¾ cup oat flour

⅓ cup oat bran
3 tablespoons date sugar
3 tablespoons vital gluten
¾ teaspoon salt
2 teaspoons yeast

SMALL

1 cup apple juice
1 tablespoon canola oil
1¾ cups whole wheat
 bread flour
½ cup oat flour

¼ cup oat bran
2 tablespoons date sugar
2 tablespoons vital gluten
½ teaspoon salt
1 teaspoon yeast

Miso Bread

Lactose-free, milk-free, low-fat

LARGE

1¾ cups water
4 cups whole wheat bread
 flour
½ cup soy flour

4 tablespoons miso paste
2 tablespoons barley malt
 sweetener
4 teaspoons yeast

MEDIUM

1⅜ cups water
3 cups whole wheat bread
 flour
⅜ cup soy flour

3 tablespoons miso paste
1⅓ tablespoons barley malt
 sweetener
3 teaspoons yeast

SMALL

⅞ cup water
2 cups whole wheat bread
 flour
¼ cup soy flour

2 tablespoons miso paste
1 tablespoon barley malt
 sweetener
2 teaspoons yeast

Nutrition Facts (based on medium-size loaf)

Serving Size 2.879 ounces (81.63g)

Servings Per Container 10

Amount Per Serving

Calories 144	Calories from Fat 15

	% Daily Value*
Total Fat 2g	3%
Saturated Fat 0g	0%
Cholesterol 0mg	0%
Sodium 192mg	0%
Total Carbohydrate 29g	10%
Dietary Fiber 2g	8%
Sugars 0g	
Protein 7g	

Vitamin A	0%	Vitamin C	0%
Calcium	2%	Iron	10%

*Percent Daily Values are based on a 2,000 calorie diet. Your daily values may be higher or lower depending on your calorie needs.

Muesli Bread

Lactose-free, milk-free, high-fiber

LARGE

1¾ cups water

2 tablespoons canola or safflower oil

4 cups whole wheat bread flour

1 cup muesli

4 tablespoons dates

1 teaspoon salt

4 teaspoons yeast

If your machine has a raisin bread cycle, add these at the beep; otherwise, add after first knead:

4 tablespoons raisins

Canola and safflower oil are good vegetable oils because they have a clean flavor that does not distract from the sweet and nutty muesli theme. Add one tablespoon of molasses or honey for extra flavor.

Nutrition Facts (based on medium-size loaf)

Serving Size 3.153 ounces (89.40g)

Servings Per Container   10

Amount Per Serving

Calories 191   Calories from Fat 32

	% *Daily Value**
Total Fat 4g	6%
Saturated Fat 1g	5%
Cholesterol 0mg	0%
Sodium 182mg	0%
Total Carbohydrate 36g	12%
Dietary Fiber 3g	12%
Sugars 6g	
Protein 9g	

| Vitamin A | 0% | Vitamin C | 0% |
| Calcium | 3% | Iron | 10% |

---

*Percent Daily Values are based on a 2,000 calorie diet. Your daily values may be higher or lower depending on your calorie needs.

MEDIUM

1⅜ cups water

1½ tablespoons canola or safflower oil

3 cups whole wheat bread flour

¾ cup muesli

3 tablespoons dates

¾ teaspoon salt

3 teaspoons yeast

If your machine has a raisin bread cycle, add these at the beep; otherwise, add after first knead:

3 tablespoons raisins

Small

7/8 cup water
1 tablespoon canola or
    safflower oil
2 cups whole wheat bread
    flour

1/2 cup muesli
2 tablespoons dates
1/2 teaspoon salt
2 teaspoons yeast

If your machine has a raisin bread cycle, add 2 tablespoons raisins at the beep; otherwise, add after first knead.

Sesame Butter Bread

Lactose-free, milk-free, high-protein

Large

1 1/2 cups soymilk
1/4 cup sesame seed butter
    (tahini)
2 cups whole wheat bread
    flour
2 cups unbleached bread
    flour

1/4 cup date sugar
3 tablespoons vital gluten
1 teaspoon salt
2 1/2 teaspoons yeast

A crunchy, crusted, high-rising loaf with a buttery, rich flavor. The sesame seed butter increases the protein quality while acting to increasing richness.

Medium

1 1/8 cups soymilk
3 tablespoons sesame seed
    butter (tahini)

3 tablespoons date sugar
2 tablespoons vital gluten
3/4 teaspoon salt

1½ cups whole wheat
  bread flour
1½ cups unbleached bread
  flour

2 teaspoons yeast

SMALL

¾ cup soymilk
2 tablespoons sesame seed
  butter (tahini)
1 cup whole wheat bread
  flour
1 cup unbleached bread
  flour

2 tablespoons date sugar
1½ tablespoons vital gluten
½ teaspoon salt
1½ teaspoons yeast

Nutrition Facts (based on medium-size loaf)
Serving Size 2.589 ounces (73.40g)
Servings Per Container   10

Amount Per Serving
Calories 180   Calories from Fat 20

	% *Daily Value**
Total Fat 2g	3%
Saturated Fat 1g	5%
Cholesterol 0mg	0%
Sodium 186mg	0%
Total Carbohydrate 34g	11%
Dietary Fiber 2g	8%
Sugars 2g	
Protein 8g	

Vitamin A 0%	Vitamin C 0%
Calcium 2%	Iron 11%

*Percent Daily Values are based on a 2,000 calorie diet. Your daily values may be higher or lower depending on your calorie needs.

Nuts About Soy

Lactose-free, milk-free, high-fiber, high-protein

LARGE

2 cups low-fat soymilk
2 tablespoons honey
2 tablespoons olive oil
4 cups whole wheat bread
    flour

½ cup soy flour
½ cup soy nuts
4 tablespoons sesame seeds
1 teaspoon salt
4 teaspoons yeast

This recipe contains three sources of soy. Soy protein contains plant estrogens that may help to alleviate the symptoms of

---

Nutrition Facts (based on medium-size loaf)

Serving Size 3.147 ounces (89.22g)

Servings Per Container   10

Amount Per Serving

Calories 206	Calories from Fat 58

	% *Daily Value**
Total Fat 6g	9%
Saturated Fat 1g	5%
Cholesterol 0mg	0%
Sodium 180mg	0%
Total Carbohydrate 32g	11%
Dietary Fiber 3g	12%
Sugars 3g	
Protein 9g	

Vitamin A 7%	Vitamin C 0%
Calcium 9%	Iron 14%

*Percent Daily Values are based on a 2,000 calorie diet. Your daily values may be higher or lower depending on your calorie needs.

menopause. Serve it as a hearty base for vegetable sandwiches
or as a complement to cold and hot soups. Try avocado and
tomato slices as a topping.

MEDIUM

1½ cups low-fat soymilk
1½ tablespoons honey
1½ tablespoons olive oil
3 cups whole wheat bread
   flour

⅜ cup soy flour
⅜ cup soy nuts
3 tablespoons sesame seeds
¾ teaspoon salt
3 teaspoons yeast

SMALL

1 cup low-fat soymilk
1 tablespoon honey
1 tablespoon olive oil
2 cups whole wheat bread
   flour

¼ cup soy flour
¼ cup soy nuts
2 tablespoons sesame seeds
½ teaspoon salt
2 teaspoons yeast

Raisin Bran Bread

Lactose-free, milk-free, high-fiber

LARGE

1⅓ cups water
2½ tablespoons canola oil
1⅓ tablespoons honey
2⅔ cups whole wheat
   bread flour
⅔ cup rice bran

⅔ cup rice flour
1½ tablespoons vital gluten
   (optional)
1 teaspoon salt
2½ teaspoons yeast

If your machine has a raisin bread cycle, add these at the beep;
otherwise, add after the first knead:

½ cup raisins

A medium-rising, chewy breakfast bread. Use the timer to
have a fresh loaf waiting for you in the morning.

MEDIUM

1 cup water
2 tablespoons canola oil
1 tablespoon honey
2 cups whole wheat bread
    flour
½ cup rice bran

½ cup rice flour
1 tablespoon vital gluten
    (optional)
¾ teaspoon salt
1½ teaspoons yeast

If your machine has a raisin bread cycle, add these at the beep; otherwise, add after the first knead:

⅓ cup raisins

Nutrition Facts (based on medium-size loaf)

Serving Size 2.589 ounces (73.39g)

Servings Per Container   10

Amount Per Serving

Calories 167   Calories from Fat 40

	% *Daily Value**
Total Fat 4g	6%
Saturated Fat 1g	5%
Cholesterol 0mg	0%
Sodium 164mg	0%
Total Carbohydrate 30g	10%
Dietary Fiber 2g	8%
Sugars 5g	
Protein 7g	

Vitamin A 0%	Vitamin C 0%
Calcium 1%	Iron 12%

---

*Percent Daily Values are based on a 2,000 calorie diet. Your daily values may be higher or lower depending on your calorie needs.

SMALL

⅔ cup water
1¼ tablespoons canola oil
2 teaspoons honey
1⅓ cups whole wheat
   bread flour
⅓ cup rice bran

⅓ cup rice flour
2 teaspoons vital gluten
   (optional)
½ teaspoon salt
1 teaspoon yeast

If your machine has a raisin bread cycle, add these at the beep; otherwise, add after the first knead:

¼ cup raisins

Garlic Herb Bread

Lactose-free, milk-free, low-fat

LARGE

2 cups water
2 tablespoons molasses
4 cups whole wheat bread
   flour
1 cup thick rolled oats

1 teaspoon dried basil
1 teaspoon dried oregano
1 teaspoon garlic powder
1 teaspoon salt
4 teaspoons yeast

A great bread to serve with spaghetti. We like to spread a bit of Better Butter (see Chapter 6 for recipe) or olive oil on top.

MEDIUM

1½ cups water
1½ tablespoons molasses
3 cups whole wheat bread
   flour
¾ cup thick rolled oats

¾ teaspoon dried basil
¾ teaspoon dried oregano
¾ teaspoon garlic powder
¾ teaspoon salt
3 teaspoons yeast

SMALL

1 cup water	½ teaspoon dried basil
1 tablespoon molasses	½ teaspoon dried oregano
2 cups whole wheat bread flour	½ teaspoon garlic powder
	½ teaspoon salt
½ cup thick rolled oats	2 teaspoons yeast

Nutrition Facts (based on medium-size loaf)

Serving Size 1.946 ounces (55.18g)

Servings Per Container   10

Amount Per Serving

Calories 102   Calories from Fat 7

	% *Daily Value**
Total Fat 1g	2%
Saturated Fat 0g	0%
Cholesterol 0mg	0%
Sodium 163mg	0%
Total Carbohydrate 21g	7%
Dietary Fiber 2g	8%
Sugars 1g	
Protein 5g	

Vitamin A	0%	Vitamin C	0%
Calcium	2%	Iron	8%

*Percent Daily Values are based on a 2,000 calorie diet. Your daily values may be higher or lower depending on your calorie needs.

Buckwheat Apple Bread

Lactose-free, milk-free, high-fiber

LARGE

1½ cups apple juice	½ cup buckwheat flour
2 eggs	4 tablespoons vital gluten
4 cups whole wheat bread flour	1 teaspoon salt
	2½ teaspoons yeast

A slightly sweet, high-rising loaf with which to start the day. This bread is excellent toasted.

Nutrition Facts (based on medium-size loaf)

Serving Size 2.846 ounces (80.68g)

Servings Per Container   10

Amount Per Serving

Calories 156   Calories from Fat 12

% *Daily Value**

Total Fat 1g	2%
Saturated Fat 0g	0%
Cholesterol 21mg	7%
Sodium 175mg	0%
Total Carbohydrate 31g	10%
Dietary Fiber 3g	12%
Sugars 0g	
Protein 9g	

Vitamin A	1%	Vitamin C	19%
Calcium	1%	Iron	10%

*Percent Daily Values are based on a 2,000 calorie diet. Your daily values may be higher or lower depending on your calorie needs.

MEDIUM

1⅛ cups apple juice
1 egg plus 1 egg white
3 cups whole wheat bread
    flour

⅓ cup buckwheat flour
3 tablespoons vital gluten
¾ teaspoon salt
2 teaspoons yeast

SMALL

¾ cup apple juice
1 egg
2 cups whole wheat bread
    flour

¼ cup buckwheat flour
2 tablespoons vital gluten
½ teaspoon salt
1½ teaspoons yeast

CHAPTER 11

Low-Fat, Cholesterol-Free, and Egg-Free Breads

Recommended for: high blood cholesterol, heart disease, weight maintenance, and egg allergy

What we commonly call fats are nutritionally considered to be lipids. Lipids are compounds that are insoluble in water. Lipids important to health include fats, oils, fatty acids, and cholesterol. Although today fat is often considered a "bad" substance, these nutrients are necessary in the diet as sources of energy, essential fatty acids, and the fat-soluble vitamins.

Fats and Bread

Fats and lipids make food more appetizing and flavorful. When added to bread, fats and oils appear to shorten the long masses of gluten, making the bread more tender. This is why they are called shortening. Fats and oils also slow the loss of water from bread by coating the starch granules. This helps to prevent the bread from becoming stale and keeps it tasting fresher for longer.

Bread is a naturally low-fat food, and the few grams of

fat that are present in some recipes are not nutritionally significant. However, some bread recipes can contain considerable amounts of oil and other fats. Usually these fats are in the form of oil, nut and seed butters, and added nuts and seeds. Although the fats found in nuts and seeds are heart-healthy, they are nevertheless a source of calories that should be limited in some individuals. Ingredients that can be substituted for fats and oils are listed later in this chapter.

Bread and Cholesterol

Individuals with familial hypercholesteremia should limit the amount of cholesterol they consume because it can cause their blood cholesterol levels to rise. Limiting cholesterol consumption can be done by eliminating eggs and butter from bread recipes. However, the amount of saturated fat and cholesterol present in a few slices of bread is not significant. The major source of saturated fat and cholesterol in bread is the butter with which many people smother the bread with after baking.

This chapter contains low-fat and cholesterol-free bread recipes for individuals who must reduce the amount of fat and cholesterol in their diets. Because eggs are a rich source of cholesterol, most of these recipes are also egg-free and suitable for individuals who are allergic to eggs.

If you wish to make low-fat breads, avoid the following ingredients:

Butter
Cheese
Cream
Egg yolks
Margarine
Mayonnaise
Nuts and nut butters
Olive oil
Seeds and seed butters

Sour cream
Tahini (sesame seed paste)
Vegetable oils
Whole milk
Yogurt

Here are some fat replacements for bread baking:

Applesauce
Banana puree
Egg replacers such as Ener-G Foods' Egg Replacer
Honey
Molasses
Nonfat yogurt
Prune puree

If you want to make low-cholesterol bread, avoid these ingredients:

Butter
Cheese
Cottage Cheese
Cream Cheese
Egg yolks
Meat fillings
Whole eggs
Whole milk
Yogurt

If you are allergic to eggs, avoid the following bread ingredients:

Eggnog
Eggs
Egg whites
Mayonnaise
Powdered eggs

Ginger Pumpkin Bread

Low-fat, cholesterol-free, high-fiber, egg-free

LARGE

1⅛ cups nonfat milk
1 cup canned pumpkin
¼ cup blackstrap molasses
2 cups whole wheat bread
   flour
2 cups unbleached bread
   flour

2 tablespoons vital gluten
1 teaspoon ginger
1 teaspoon salt
2 teaspoons yeast

A moist, high-rising bread that keeps well. It is moist and rich due to the molasses.

Nutrition Facts (based on medium-size loaf)

Serving Size 2.957 ounces (83.82g)
Servings Per Container   10

Amount Per Serving

Calories 166   Calories from Fat 10

	% *Daily Value**
Total Fat 1g	2%
Saturated Fat 0g	0%
Cholesterol 0mg	0%
Sodium 177mg	0%
Total Carbohydrate 34g	11%
Dietary Fiber 2g	8%
Sugars 3g	
Protein 7g	

Vitamin A 44%	Vitamin C 1%
Calcium 7%	Iron 16%

*Percent Daily Values are based on a 2,000 calorie diet. Your daily values may be higher or lower depending on your calorie needs.

Medium

¾ cup nonfat milk
¾ cup canned pumpkin
3 tablespoons blackstrap
 molasses
1½ cups whole wheat
 bread flour

1½ cups unbleached bread
 flour
1½ tablespoons vital gluten
¾ teaspoon ginger
¾ teaspoon salt
1½ teaspoons yeast

Small

½ cup nonfat milk
½ cup canned pumpkin
2 tablespoons blackstrap
 molasses
1 cup whole wheat bread
 flour

1 cup unbleached bread
 flour
1 tablespoon vital gluten
½ teaspoon ginger
½ teaspoon salt
1 teaspoon yeast

Honey Graham Bread

Low-fat, cholesterol-free, high-fiber, egg-free

Large

1¾ cups water
3 tablespoons honey
2½ cups whole wheat
 bread flour
1½ cups graham flour

½ cup nonfat milk powder
4 tablespoons vital gluten
1 teaspoon salt
2½ teaspoons yeast

A medium-rising, slightly sweet bread. Contrasts wonderfully
with bean spreads.

Medium

1⅓ cups water
2 tablespoons honey
2 cups whole wheat bread
 flour
1 cup graham flour

⅓ cup nonfat milk powder
3 tablespoons vital gluten
¾ teaspoon salt
2 teaspoons yeast

SMALL

⅞ cup water
1 tablespoon honey
1½ cups whole wheat
    bread flour
¾ cup graham flour

¼ cup nonfat milk powder
2 tablespoons vital gluten
½ teaspoon salt
1½ teaspoons yeast

Nutrition Facts (based on medium-size loaf)

Serving Size 2.749 ounces (77.92g)

Servings Per Container   10

Amount Per Serving

Calories 142   Calories from Fat 7

	% *Daily Value**
Total Fat 1g	2%
Saturated Fat 0g	0%
Cholesterol 0mg	0%
Sodium 176mg	0%
Total Carbohydrate 30g	10%
Dietary Fiber 3g	12%
Sugars 4g	
Protein 8g	

Vitamin A	1%	Vitamin C	0%
Calcium	4%	Iron	9%

---

*Percent Daily Values are based on a 2,000 calorie diet. Your daily values may be higher or lower depending on your calorie needs.

Crunchy Banana Yogurt Bread

Low-fat, cholesterol-free, high-fiber, egg-free

LARGE

1 cup nonfat milk
1 cup mashed banana
¾ cup nonfat yogurt

1 cup whole wheat bread
    flour
1 cup garbanzo bean flour

3 tablespoons almond
   extract
2 cups unbleached bread
   flour

¼ cup poppyseeds
2 tablespoons vital gluten
1 teaspoon salt
2 teaspoons yeast

A very light, sweet bread with a slight crunch of poppyseeds. If you are just introducing the family to whole grains, this is a good bread to start with.

MEDIUM

¾ cup nonfat milk
¾ cup mashed banana
½ cup nonfat yogurt

¾ cup whole wheat bread
   flour
¾ cup garbanzo bean flour

Nutrition Facts (based on medium-size loaf)

Serving Size 3.480 ounces (98.65g)

Servings Per Container   10

Amount Per Serving

Calories 171	Calories from Fat 19

	% Daily Value*
Total Fat 2g	3%
Saturated Fat 0g	0%
Cholesterol 1mg	0%
Sodium 185mg	0%
Total Carbohydrate 32g	11%
Dietary Fiber 1g	4%
Sugars 1g	
Protein 9g	

Vitamin A 1%	Vitamin C 2%
Calcium 10%	Iron 9%

---

*Percent Daily Values are based on a 2,000 calorie diet. Your daily values may be higher or lower depending on your calorie needs.

2½ tablespoons almond
   extract
1½ cups unbleached bread
   flour

3 tablespoons poppyseeds
1½ tablespoons vital gluten
¾ teaspoon salt
1½ teaspoons yeast

SMALL

½ cup nonfat milk
½ cup mashed banana
⅓ cup nonfat yogurt
2 tablespoons almond
   extract
1 cup unbleached bread
   flour

½ cup whole wheat bread
   flour
½ cup garbanzo bean flour
2 tablespoons poppyseeds
1 tablespoon vital gluten
½ teaspoon salt
1 teaspoon yeast

Oat Bran Bread

Low-fat, high-fiber, egg-free

LARGE

1⅞ cups nonfat milk
2 cups whole wheat bread
   flour
2 cups enriched bread flour
⅔ cup oat bran

¼ cup date sugar
4 tablespoons vital gluten
1 teaspoon salt
2½ teaspoons yeast

A good basic bread recipe. The soluble fiber in this bread makes it a good choice for people at risk for heart disease. For a tender crust, brush milk on top of the unbaked loaf just before the bake cycle starts (see Chapter 6).

MEDIUM

1½ cups nonfat milk
1½ cups whole wheat
   bread flour
1½ cups enriched bread
   flour

½ cup oat bran
3 tablespoons date sugar
2 tablespoons vital gluten
¾ teaspoon salt
2 teaspoons yeast

SMALL

1 cup nonfat milk	2 tablespoons date sugar
1 cup whole wheat bread flour	1 tablespoon vital gluten
1 cup enriched bread flour	½ teaspoon salt
⅓ cup oat bran	1½ teaspoons yeast

Nutrition Facts (based on medium-size loaf)

Serving Size 2.583 ounces (73.24g)

Servings Per Container   10

Amount Per Serving

Calories 127   Calories from Fat 7

	% *Daily Value**
Total Fat 1g	2%
Saturated Fat 0g	0%
Cholesterol 1mg	0%
Sodium 127mg	0%
Total Carbohydrate 26g	9%
Dietary Fiber 2g	8%
Sugars 3g	
Protein 7g	

Vitamin A	2%	Vitamin C	0%
Calcium	5%	Iron	8%

---

*Percent Daily Values are based on a 2,000 calorie diet. Your daily values may be higher or lower depending on your calorie needs.

Prune Amaranth Bread

Low-fat, high-protein, egg-free

LARGE

1⅔ cups water
2 cups whole wheat bread
  flour
1½ cups unbleached white
  flour
½ cup amaranth flour

½ cup nonfat dry milk
3 tablespoons date sugar
2 tablespoons vital gluten
1 teaspoon salt
2 teaspoons yeast

If your machine has a raisin bread cycle, add ¾ cup pitted prunes at the beep; otherwise, add after first knead.

A high-rising, sweet loaf. The amaranth and milk add to its protein quality.

MEDIUM

1¼ cups water
1½ cups whole wheat
  bread flour
1⅛ cups unbleached white
  flour
⅓ cup amaranth flour

⅓ cup nonfat dry milk
2½ tablespoons date sugar
1½ tablespoons vital gluten
¾ teaspoon salt
1½ teaspoons yeast

If your machine has a raisin bread cycle, add ½ cup pitted prunes at the beep; otherwise, add after first knead.

SMALL

⅞ cup water
1 cup whole wheat bread
  flour
¾ cup unbleached white
  flour
¼ cup amaranth flour

¼ cup dry milk
1½ tablespoons date sugar
1 tablespoon vital gluten
½ teaspoon salt
1 teaspoon yeast

If your machine has a raisin bread cycle, add ⅓ cup pitted prunes at the beep; otherwise, add after first knead.

Nutrition Facts (based on medium-size loaf)

Serving Size 2.969 ounces (84.18g)

Servings Per Container   10

Amount Per Serving

Calories 168   Calories from Fat 7

	% *Daily Value**
Total Fat 1g	2%
Saturated Fat 0g	0%
Cholesterol 0mg	0%
Sodium 175mg	0%
Total Carbohydrate 35g	12%
Dietary Fiber 2g	8%
Sugars 5g	
Protein 8g	

Vitamin A 3%	Vitamin C 1%
Calcium 4%	Iron 10%

---

*Percent Daily Values are based on a 2,000 calorie diet. Your daily values may be higher or lower depending on your calorie needs.

Molasses Wheat Bread

Low-fat, high-fiber, lactose-free, milk-free, egg-free

LARGE

1½ cups nonfat soymilk
⅜ cup molasses
4 cups whole wheat bread flour
4 tablespoons rice polish
4 tablespoons thick rolled oats

4 tablespoons vital gluten
1 teaspoon salt
4 teaspoons yeast
⅔ cup chopped prunes

The molasses and rice polish lend a dark color, and the prunes add moisture and delightful richness to this whole wheat bread.

MEDIUM

1⅛ cups nonfat soymilk
¼ cup molasses
3 cups whole wheat bread
   flour
3 tablespoons rice polish
3 tablespoons thick rolled
   oats

3 tablespoons vital gluten
¾ teaspoon salt
3 teaspoons yeast
½ cup chopped prunes

Nutrition Facts (based on medium-size loaf)

Serving Size 3.019 ounces (85.58g)
Servings Per Container   10

Amount Per Serving

Calories 188   Calories from Fat 10

	% Daily Value*
Total Fat 1g	2%
Saturated Fat 0g	0%
Cholesterol 0mg	0%
Sodium 194mg	0%
Total Carbohydrate 40g	13%
Dietary Fiber 3g	12%
Sugars 7g	
Protein 10g	

Vitamin A 1%	Vitamin C 0%
Calcium 8%	Iron 20%

---

*Percent Daily Values are based on a 2,000 calorie diet. Your daily values may be higher or lower depending on your calorie needs.

SMALL

⅞ cup nonfat soymilk
3 tablespoons molasses
2 cups whole wheat bread
   flour
2 tablespoons rice polish
2 tablespoons thick rolled
   oats

2 tablespoons vital gluten
½ teaspoon salt
2 teaspoons yeast
⅓ cup chopped prunes

Multigrain Soy Bread

Low-fat, milk-free, lactose-free, high-fiber, egg-free

LARGE

1½ cups lowfat vanilla
   soymilk
2 tablespoons honey
2 cups spelt flour
1 cup oat flour
1 cup unbleached bread
   flour

⅓ cup rice polish
3 tablespoons vital gluten
1 teaspoon salt
2 teaspoons yeast

This is a very high-rising, golden loaf. The spelt, oats, and rice are whole grains that combine nicely with the refined white flour. If your family is just making the transition from refined grains to whole grains, this is a good bread to start with. If you like, substitute all or part of the white flour with whole grain wheat and increase the gluten to 4 tablespoons.

MEDIUM

1⅛ cups lowfat vanilla
   soymilk
1½ tablespoons honey
1½ cups spelt flour
¾ cup oat flour
¾ cup unbleached bread
   flour

¼ cup rice polish
2 tablespoons vital gluten
¾ teaspoon salt
1½ teaspoons yeast

SMALL

¾ cup lowfat vanilla
   soymilk
1 tablespoon honey

3 tablespoons rice polish
1½ tablespoons vital gluten
½ teaspoon salt

Nutrition Facts (based on medium-size loaf)

Serving Size 2.462 ounces (69.80g)

Servings Per Container   10

Amount Per Serving

Calories 156   Calories from Fat 11

	% *Daily Value**
Total Fat 1g	2%
Saturated Fat 0g	0%
Cholesterol 0mg	0%
Sodium 186mg	0%
Total Carbohydrate 32g	11%
Dietary Fiber 2g	8%
Sugars 3g	
Protein 9g	

Vitamin A 0%	Vitamin C 0%
Calcium 2%	Iron 11%

---

*Percent Daily Values are based on a 2,000 calorie diet. Your daily values may be higher or lower depending on your calorie needs.

1 cup spelt flour
½ cup oat flour
½ cup unbleached bread
  flour

1 teaspoon yeast

Buckwheat Prune Bread

Low-fat, lactose-free, milk-free, high-fiber

LARGE

1½ cups prune juice
2 eggs
4 cups whole wheat bread
  flour

½ cup buckwheat flour
4 tablespoons vital gluten
1 teaspoon salt
2½ teaspoons yeast

Nutrition Facts (based on medium-size loaf)

Serving Size 3.292 ounces (93.32g)
Servings Per Container   10

Amount Per Serving

Calories 192   Calories from Fat 13

                                    % *Daily Value**

Total Fat 1g	2%
Saturated Fat 0g	0%
Cholesterol 21mg	7%
Sodium 176mg	0%
Total Carbohydrate 40g	13%
Dietary Fiber 4g	16%
Sugars 9g	
Protein 10g	

Vitamin A	3%	Vitamin C 2%
Calcium	2%	Iron 13%

---

*Percent Daily Values are based on a 2,000 calorie diet. Your daily values may be higher or lower depending on your calorie needs.

If your machine has a raisin bread cycle, add this at the beep; otherwise, add after first knead:

1 cup chopped, pitted
  prunes

This rich, slightly sweet bread goes great with a cup of herbal tea in the afternoon. It will supply your body with iron and protein and keep it energized the rest of the day.

MEDIUM

1⅛ cups prune juice	⅓ cup buckwheat flour
1 egg and 1 egg white	3 tablespoons vital gluten
3 cups whole wheat bread	¾ teaspoon salt
flour	2 teaspoons yeast

If your machine has a raisin bread cycle, add this at the beep; otherwise, add after first knead:

¾ cup chopped, pitted
  prunes

SMALL

¾ cup prune juice	¼ cup buckwheat flour
1 egg	2 tablespoons vital gluten
2 cups whole wheat bread	½ teaspoon salt
flour	1½ teaspoons yeast

If your machine has a raisin bread cycle, add this at the beep; otherwise, add after first knead:

½ cup chopped, pitted
  prunes.

Raisin Pumpkin Bread

Low-fat, milk-free, lactose-free, egg-free

LARGE

1 cup nonfat soymilk
1 cup cannned pumpkin
4 tablespoons honey
2 cups whole wheat bread
  flour

2 cups spelt flour
1 tablespoon vital gluten
½ teaspoon ginger
1 teaspoon salt
2 teaspoons yeast

If your machine has a raisin bread cycle, add this at the beep; otherwise, add after first knead:

1 cup sultana raisins

Nutrition Facts (based on medium-size loaf)
Serving Size 3.309 ounces (93.80g)
Servings Per Container   10

Amount Per Serving

Calories 201   Calories from Fat 10

		% *Daily Value**
Total Fat 1g		2%
Saturated Fat 0g		0%
Cholesterol 0mg		0%
Sodium 173mg		0%
Total Carbohydrate 43g		14%
Dietary Fiber 4g		16%
Sugars 6g		
Protein 7g		

Vitamin A 41%	Vitamin C 2%
Calcium 4%	Iron 11%

---

*Percent Daily Values are based on a 2,000 calorie diet. Your daily values may be higher or lower depending on your calorie needs.

Another favorite. This spicy bread gets its moistness not from fat but from the pumpkin and honey. It is full of beta carotene from the pumpkin and not overly sweet.

MEDIUM

¾ cup nonfat soymilk
¾ cup cannned pumpkin
3 tablespoons honey
1½ cups whole wheat
   bread flour

1½ cups spelt flour
¾ tablespoon vital gluten
⅓ teaspoon ginger
¾ teaspoon salt
1½ teaspoons yeast

If your machine has a raisin bread cycle, add this at the beep; otherwise, add after first knead:

¾ cup sultana raisins

SMALL

½ cup nonfat soymilk
½ cup cannned pumpkin
2 tablespoons honey
1 cup whole wheat bread
   flour

1 cup spelt flour
½ tablespoon vital gluten
¼ teaspoon ginger
½ teaspoon salt
1 teaspoon yeast

If your machine has a raisin bread cycle, add this at the beep; otherwise, add after first knead:

½ cup sultana raisins

CHAPTER 12

Low-Sodium and Low-Salt Breads

Recommended for: hypertension, edema due to water retention, heart failure, kidney failure

Sodium and potassium are major components of all bodily fluids. Sodium is the major mineral found in the fluid outside of cells, and potassium is the major mineral found in the fluid inside of cells. The body usually maintains tight control over the concentrations of these minerals. When the mechanism responsible for this regulation fails, the result is an imbalance of fluid volumes in the body, resulting in high blood pressure and cardiovascular problems. Dietary control over the amount of sodium, sodium chloride (salt), and potassium that is eaten is often recommended for people who have heart failure, kidney failure, edema, or salt-sensitive high blood pressure. The recommendation is usually to eat less sodium or salt-containing foods.

Salt in the American Diet

In the American diet, the greatest single source of sodium is salt. The average American consumes between four thousand

153

and six thousand milligrams of sodium a day, although the body needs no more than several hundred milligrams of sodium a day to function. Since each teaspoon of salt contains about two thousand milligrams of sodium, the easiest way to reduce sodium and salt intake is to eliminate or greatly reduce the use of table salt.

Salt and Bread

In making yeasted breads, salt is traditionally used to inhibit protein-digesting enzymes that weaken gluten structure. It is also used to inhibit the action of the yeast, preventing overgrowth and a dough with uneven air pockets. However, in bread machines, salt affects little more than taste. Removing the salt from any whole grain recipe only slightly affects bread height.

Sodium and Bread

Most of the recipes in this book are low-sodium. However, if your physician recommends a more severe sodium restriction, it may be necessary to use low-sodium milk. If you are also on a protein-restricted diet, the protein content of the recipes can also be reduced by using all-purpose flour instead of the higher protein bread flour. The gluten may also be omitted and juice or nut milks substituted for higher protein cow's milk and soymilk.

If you are on a low-salt or low-sodium diet, you can use these ingredients:

Extracts such as almond, vanilla, walnut
Garlic (fresh, dried, juiced)
Ginger (fresh, candied, juice or powder)
Grated lemon and orange rind (organic fruit only)
Herbs (dried or fresh)
Lemon juice
Lime juice

Onion (fresh, dried, juice)
Sodium-free baking powder
Spices and seasonings identified as powders, e.g., garlic powder, celery powder
Unsalted butter

Avoid these bread ingredients if you are salt sensitive:

Butter (salted)
Salt
Sea salt
Seasoning salts such as garlic salt, onion salt, celery salt

Avoid these ingredients to limit your sodium intake:

Baking powder (regular)
Baking soda (sodium bicarbonate)
Butter (salted)
Buttermilk
Ingredients containing sodium citrate, a preservative
Salt
Sea salt
Seasoning salts such as garlic salt, onion salt, celery salt
Seasonings containing monosodium glutamate (MSG)
Tomato juice

Low-Sodium Bran Bread

Very low-sodium, lactose-free, milk-free, high-fiber

LARGE

1⅔ cups unflavored
   soymilk or apple juice
4 cups whole wheat bread
   flour

⅓ cup oat bran
3 tablespoons date sugar
4 tablespoons vital gluten
3 teaspoons yeast

This recipe is for those who must restrict their intake of sodium. Each slice contains 17 mg of sodium per half-inch slice.

If you are on a moderately restricted low-sodium diet, you can add ¼ teaspoon of salt to the medium recipe. This will produce a half-inch slice containing 125 milligrams of sodium.

If you are also on a protein-restricted diet, substitute all-purpose white flour for half of the whole wheat flour, all-purpose whole wheat flour for the whole wheat bread flour, and apple juice for the soymilk and eliminate the gluten.

MEDIUM

1¼ cups unflavored
    soymilk or apple juice
3 cups whole wheat bread
    flour

¼ cup oat bran
2¼ tablespoons date sugar
3 tablespoons vital gluten
2 teaspoons yeast

Nutrition Facts (based on medium-size loaf)

Serving Size 2.658 ounces (75.36g)
Servings Per Container 10

Amount Per Serving	
Calories 153	Calories from Fat 14

	% Daily Value*
Total Fat 2g	3%
Saturated Fat 0g	0%
Cholesterol 0mg	0%
Sodium 17mg	0%
Total Carbohydrate 31g	10%
Dietary Fiber 3g	12%
Sugars 2g	
Protein 9g	

Vitamin A	6%	Vitamin C	0%
Calcium	5%	Iron	10%

*Percent Daily Values are based on a 2,000 calorie diet. Your daily values may be higher or lower depending on your calorie needs.

SMALL

⅞ cup unflavored soymilk
  or apple juice
2 cups whole wheat bread
  flour

3 tablespoons oat bran
1½ tablespoons date sugar
2 tablespoons vital gluten
1½ teaspoons yeast

Low-Sodium Herb Bread

Very low-sodium

LARGE

1½ cups low-sodium milk
2 tablespoons virgin olive
  oil
2 tablespoons honey
2 cups whole wheat bread
  flour
2 cups unbleached bread
  flour

3 tablespoons dried herbs
2 tablespoons vital gluten
1½ tablespoons dried
  lemon peel
2 teaspoons yeast

This is a sodium-free bread. Each half-inch slice contains only 2 milligrams of sodium. Low-sodium milk is often available in supermarkets or at health-food stores.

MEDIUM

1 cup low-sodium milk
1½ tablespoons virgin olive
  oil
1½ tablespoons honey
1½ cups whole wheat
  bread flour
1½ cups unbleached bread
  flour

2 tablespoons dried herbs
1½ tablespoons vital gluten
1 tablespoon dried lemon
  peel
1½ teaspoons yeast

SMALL

¾ cup low-sodium milk
1 tablespoon virgin olive
  oil
1 tablespoon honey
1 cup whole wheat bread
  flour
1 cup unbleached bread
  flour

1½ tablespoons dried herbs
1 tablespoon vital gluten
¾ tablespoon dried lemon
  peel
1 teaspoon yeast

Nutrition Facts (based on medium-size loaf)

Serving Size 2.496 ounces (70.77g)
Servings Per Container   10

Amount Per Serving

Calories 178   Calories from Fat 32

	% Daily Value*
Total Fat 4g	6%
Saturated Fat 1g	5%
Cholesterol 3mg	1%
Sodium 2mg	0%
Total Carbohydrate 31g	10%
Dietary Fiber 2g	8%
Sugars 4g	
Protein 7g	

Vitamin A	1%	Vitamin C	1%
Calcium	3%	Iron	9%

*Percent Daily Values are based on a 2,000 calorie diet. Your daily values may be higher or lower depending on your calorie needs.

Garlic Bread

Low-sodium

LARGE

1½ cups low-sodium milk
3 tablespoons extra virgin
    olive oil
2 cups whole wheat bread
    flour

2 cups unbleached bread
    flour
1 tablespoon garlic powder
3 tablespoons gluten
2 teaspoons yeast

For a delicious tender crust, brush unbaked top of loaf with olive oil and sprinkle generously with a nonsalt Italian seasoning.

Nutrition Facts (based on medium-size loaf)
Serving Size 2.535 ounces (71.88g)
Servings Per Container   10

Amount Per Serving

Calories 178   Calories from Fat 39

                              % Daily Value*

Total Fat 4g	6%
Saturated Fat 1g	5%
Cholesterol 4mg	1%
Sodium 3mg	0%
Total Carbohydrate 29g	10%
Dietary Fiber 2g	8%
Sugars 1g	
Protein 8g	

Vitamin A	1%	Vitamin C	0%
Calcium	3%	Iron	9%

---

*Percent Daily Values are based on a 2,000 calorie diet. Your daily values may be higher or lower depending on your calorie needs.

MEDIUM

1⅛ cups low-sodium milk
2 tablespoons extra virgin
 olive oil
1½ cups whole wheat
 bread flour
1½ cups unbleached bread
 flour

¾ tablespoon garlic
 powder
2 tablespoons gluten
1½ teaspoons yeast

SMALL

¾ cup low-sodium milk
1½ tablespoons extra virgin
 olive oil
1 cup whole wheat bread
 flour
1 cup unbleached bread
 flour

½ tablespoon garlic
 powder
1 tablespoon gluten
1 teaspoon yeast

Low-Sodium Wheat Bread

Low-sodium, lactose-free, milk-free

LARGE

1½ cups apple juice
2 tablespoons canola oil
4 cups whole wheat bread
 flour

4 tablespoons vital gluten
2½ teaspoons yeast

This is a nice sandwich bread that slices and keeps well. It contains only 56 milligrams of sodium per half-inch slice.

MEDIUM

1 cup apple juice
1½ tablespoons canola oil
3 cups whole wheat bread
 flour

3 tablespoons vital gluten
2 teaspoons yeast

SMALL

¾ cup apple juice

1 tablespoon canola oil

2 cups whole wheat bread
  flour

2 tablespoons vital gluten

1½ teaspoons yeast

Nutrition Facts (based on medium-size loaf)

Serving Size 2.355 ounces (66.77g)

Servings Per Container   10

Amount Per Serving

Calories 150   Calories from Fat 26

% *Daily Value**

Total Fat 3g	5%
Saturated Fat 0g	0%
Cholesterol 0mg	0%
Sodium 56mg	0%
Total Carbohydrate 28g	9%
Dietary Fiber 2g	8%
Sugars 3g	
Protein 8g	

Vitamin A	0%	Vitamin C	0%
Calcium	1%	Iron	9%

*Percent Daily Values are based on a 2,000 calorie diet. Your daily values may be higher or lower depending on your calorie needs.

Oatmeal Date Bread

Very low-sodium, high-fiber

LARGE

1¾ cups water
2 tablespoons canola oil
2 tablespoons honey
4 cups whole wheat bread flour
½ cup dates, whole or chopped

½ cup steel-cut oats
2 tablespoons nonfat dry milk
4 teaspoons yeast

This a great recipe to try in the morning. Set your timer and awake to the aroma of fresh bread. The dates and honey give the bread a moist texture.

Nutrition Facts (based on medium-size loaf)
Serving Size 3.175 ounces (90.01g)
Servings Per Container   10

Amount Per Serving
Calories 200   Calories from Fat 29

	% Daily Value*
Total Fat 3g	5%
Saturated Fat 0g	0%
Cholesterol 0mg	0%
Sodium 17mg	0%
Total Carbohydrate 38g	13%
Dietary Fiber 3g	12%
Sugars 7g	
Protein 8g	

Vitamin A 1%	Vitamin C 0%
Calcium 4%	Iron 10%

*Percent Daily Values are based on a 2,000 calorie diet. Your daily values may be higher or lower depending on your calorie needs.

MEDIUM

1⅜ cups water
1⅓ tablespoons canola oil
1⅓ tablespoons honey
3 cups whole wheat bread
   flour
⅜ cup dates, whole or
   chopped

⅜ cup steel-cut oats
1½ tablespoons nonfat dry
   milk
3 teaspoons yeast

SMALL

⅞ cup water
1 tablespoon canola oil
1 tablespoon honey
2 cups whole wheat bread
   flour
¼ cup dates, whole or
   chopped

¼ cup steel-cut oats
1 tablespoon nonfat dry
   milk
2 teaspoons yeast

Pizza Bread

Low-sodium, high-protein

LARGE

1¾ cups water
½ cup tomato sauce
2 tablespoons olive oil
2 teaspoons low-sodium
   soy sauce
3 cups whole wheat bread
   flour

1 cup kamut flour
¼ cup grated parmesan
   cheese
2 tablespoons date sugar
1 teaspoon dried oregano
4 teaspoons yeast

Kids love this bread, which becomes a meal with a little melted cheese and sliced tomatoes. If you cannot find kamut, substitute an equal amount of whole wheat bread flour.

MEDIUM

1⅜ cups water
⅜ cup tomato sauce
1⅓ tablespoons olive oil
1½ teaspoons low-sodium
  soy sauce
2 cups whole wheat bread
  flour

¾ cup kamut flour
3 tablespoons grated
  parmesan cheese
1⅓ tablespoons date sugar
¾ teaspoon dried oregano
3 teaspoons yeast

SMALL

⅞ cup water
¼ cup tomato sauce
1 tablespoon olive oil

½ cup kamut flour
2 tablespoons grated
  parmesan cheese

Nutrition Facts (based on medium-size loaf)

Serving Size 2.989 ounces (84.74g)
Servings Per Container   10

Amount Per Serving	
Calories 157	Calories from Fat 30

	% Daily Value*
Total Fat 3g	5%
Saturated Fat 1g	5%
Cholesterol 1mg	0%
Sodium 70mg	0%
Total Carbohydrate 27g	9%
Dietary Fiber 2g	8%
Sugars 1g	
Protein 7g	

Vitamin A	1%	Vitamin C	1%
Calcium	3%	Iron	9%

*Percent Daily Values are based on a 2,000 calorie diet. Your daily values may be higher or lower depending on your calorie needs.

1 teaspoon low-sodium soy
  sauce
1½ cups whole wheat
  bread flour

1 tablespoon date sugar
½ teaspoon dried oregano
2 teaspoons yeast

Spelt Soy Bread

Very low-sodium, milk-free, lactose-free

LARGE

1½ cups plain soymilk
2 tablespoons canola oil
2 cups whole wheat bread
  flour

2 cups spelt flour
¼ cup date sugar
3 tablespoons vital gluten
2 teaspoons yeast

Nutrition Facts (based on medium-size loaf)
Serving Size 2.544 ounces (72.13g)
Servings Per Container   10

Amount Per Serving
Calories 169   Calories from Fat 32

% *Daily Value**

Total Fat 4g	6%
Saturated Fat 0g	0%
Cholesterol 0mg	0%
Sodium 5mg	0%
Total Carbohydrate 29g	10%
Dietary Fiber 4g	16%
Sugars 3g	
Protein 8g	

Vitamin A 0%	Vitamin C	0%
Calcium 0%	Iron	10%

*Percent Daily Values are based on a 2,000 calorie diet. Your daily values may be higher or lower depending on your calorie needs.

A soft, light, high bread due to spelt. Make sure to read the label on the soymilk that you buy. Some soymilks contain added salt.

MEDIUM

1⅛ cups plain soymilk
1½ tablespoons canola oil
1½ cups whole wheat
   bread flour

1½ cups spelt flour
3 tablespoons date sugar
2 tablespoons vital gluten
1½ teaspoons yeast

SMALL

¾ cup plain soymilk
1 tablespoon canola oil
1 cup whole wheat bread
   flour

1 cup spelt flour
2 tablespoons date sugar
1 tablespoon vital gluten
1 teaspoon yeast

Sunflower Bread

Low-sodium, lactose-free, milk-free

LARGE

1⅓ cups water
2⅔ tablespoons canola oil
2⅔ tablespoons honey
3 cups whole wheat bread
   flour
⅔ cup oats

¾ cup millet
⅔ cup unsalted, toasted
   sunflower seeds
¼ cup raisins
¼ teaspoon salt
4 teaspoons yeast

A crunchy, sweet, chewy bread that kids of all ages love. Toast it for a special treat.

MEDIUM

1 cup water
2 tablespoons canola oil
2 tablespoons honey

½ cup millet
½ cup unsalted, toasted
   sunflower seeds

2 cups whole wheat bread
   flour
½ cup oats

SMALL

⅔ cup water
1⅓ tablespoons canola oil
1⅓ tablespoons honey
1½ cups whole wheat
   bread flour
⅓ cup oats

3 tablespoons raisins
⅛ + teaspoon salt
3 teaspoons yeast

⅓ cup millet
⅓ cup unsalted, toasted
   sunflower seeds
2 tablespoons raisins
⅛ teaspoon salt
2 teaspoons yeast

Nutrition Facts (based on medium-size loaf)
Serving Size 2.845 ounces (80.66g)
Servings Per Container   10

Amount Per Serving
Calories 224   Calories from Fat 67

	% Daily Value*
Total Fat 7g	11%
Saturated Fat 1g	5%
Cholesterol 0mg	0%
Sodium 29mg	0%
Total Carbohydrate 34g	11%
Dietary Fiber 4g	16%
Sugars 6g	
Protein 8g	

Vitamin A	0%	Vitamin C	0%
Calcium	2%	Iron	11%

---

*Percent Daily Values are based on a 2,000 calorie diet. Your daily values may be higher or lower depending on your calorie needs.

Honey Cornmeal Bread

Very low-sodium, high-fiber, lactose-free, milk-free

LARGE

1⅓ cups water
1⅓ tablespoons olive oil
2 tablespoons honey
⅔ cup cornmeal
⅓ cup wheat germ

½ cup flaxseeds
3 cups whole wheat bread
   flour
1 teaspoon cumin
2½ teaspoons yeast

A summer favorite. Add ⅛ teaspoon of cayenne pepper or fresh chili peppers for a spicy picnic bread.

Nutrition Facts (based on medium-size loaf)

Serving Size 2.401 ounces (68.06g)

Servings Per Container   10

Amount Per Serving

Calories 146   Calories from Fat 22

	% *Daily Value**
Total Fat 2g	3%
Saturated Fat 0g	0%
Cholesterol 0mg	0%
Sodium 6mg	0%
Total Carbohydrate 27g	9%
Dietary Fiber 3g	12%
Sugars 3g	
Protein 8g	

Vitamin A	0%	Vitamin C	0%
Calcium	1%	Iron	9%

---

*Percent Daily Values are based on a 2,000 calorie diet. Your daily values may be higher or lower depending on your calorie needs.

MEDIUM

1 cup water
1 tablespoon olive oil
1½ tablespoons honey
½ cup cornmeal
¼ cup wheat germ

⅓ cup flaxseeds
2¼ cups whole wheat
  bread flour
¾ teaspoon cumin
2 teaspoons yeast

SMALL

⅔ cup water
2 teaspoons olive oil
1 tablespoon honey
⅓ cup cornmeal
2½ tablespoons wheat
  germ

¼ cup flaxseeds
1½ cups whole wheat
  bread flour
½ teaspoon cumin
1 teaspoon yeast

Cinnamon Yogurt Bread

Low-sodium, high-fiber, high-protein

LARGE

1⅓ cups yogurt
⅔ cup water
4 tablespoons olive oil
4 tablespoons honey
4 cups whole wheat bread
  flour

⅔ cup sesame seeds
½ cup rice polish
3 tablespoons date sugar
1¼ teaspoons cinnamon
1¼ teaspoons nutmeg
4 teaspoons yeast

This is one of our favorite recipes. A dark, moist, hearty loaf with a little crunch, which you'll enjoy again and again.

MEDIUM

1 cup yogurt
½ cup water
3 tablespoons olive oil

½ cup sesame seeds
⅜ cup rice polish
2 tablespoons date sugar

3 tablespoons honey
3 cups whole wheat bread
   flour

1 teaspoon cinnamon
1 teaspoon nutmeg
3 teaspoons yeast

SMALL

⅔ cup yogurt
⅓ cup water
2 tablespoons olive oil
2 tablespoons honey
2 cups whole wheat bread
   flour

⅓ cup sesame seeds
¼ cup rice polish
1½ tablespoons date sugar
¾ teaspoon cinnamon
¾ teaspoon nutmeg
2 teaspoons yeast

Nutrition Facts (based on medium-size loaf)
Serving Size 3.379 ounces (95.81g)
Servings Per Container   10

Amount Per Serving

Calories 248	Calories from Fat 80

	% *Daily Value**
Total Fat 9g	14%
Saturated Fat 1g	5%
Cholesterol 1mg	0%
Sodium 19mg	0%
Total Carbohydrate 38g	13%
Dietary Fiber 4g	16%
Sugars 7g	
Protein 9g	

Vitamin A 0%	Vitamin C 0%
Calcium 13%	Iron 18%

---

*Percent Daily Values are based on a 2,000 calorie diet. Your daily values may be higher or lower depending on your calorie needs.

Milk-Free Breads

Recommended for: milk allergy

Milk provides proteins, which contribute to the structure of the bread; fats, which act as leavening agents; and vitamins and minerals, which increase the nutritional value of the bread. However, some people cannot consume milk because they are allergic to one or more of the proteins found in it. When these individuals drink even small amounts of milk, they experience symptoms ranging from a stuffy nose to severe gastrointestinal distress. Although milk allergy seems to have become more common in recent years, it was first described by Hippocrates (460 to 370 B.C.), who noticed stomach upset and hives as a result of drinking cow's milk.

Bread and Milk Allergy

If you have a milk allergy, your only recourse is to totally avoid all cow's milk and cow's milk–containing products and pre-pared foods. Since cow's milk can hide under a variety of

171

names in store-bought bread, baking your own bread is one way you can be sure to avoid an allergic reaction.

Some individuals who are allergic to cow's milk are able to tolerate goat's milk. Be aware, however, that the proteins in these two milks are very similar, and an allergy to one can mean an allergy to the other. Goat's milk can be purchased at health-food stores.

Substitutions for Milk

Individuals who do not or cannot drink milk are at risk for calcium, vitamin D, and riboflavin deficiencies. Soymilk that has been fortified with calcium and vitamin D is the best substitute for milk in bread. It provides protein, sugar, and fats in proportions similar to those in milk, and it can be purchased in skim, 1 percent, 2 percent, and whole-fat versions. Since soymilk is a vegetable product, it is naturally low in saturated fat and free of cholesterol.

Grain beverages such as amasake or Rice Dream can be successfully substituted for milk in bread. So can nut milks made by blending nuts and water in a blender. However, these beverages are not the nutritional equivalent of milk.

If you are allergic to milk, do not use these bread ingredients:

Butter
Casein
Caseinate
Cheese, cottage cheese
Chocolate
Half and half, coffee cream
Heavy cream, whipping cream
Lactose
Milk (whole, skim, 1 percent, 2 percent, buttermilk, sweet
    acidophilus, evaporated, condensed)
Nonfat milk solids

Powdered dry milk (whole, nonfat, buttermilk)
Sodium caseinate
Sour cream
Whey
Yogurt

If you are allergic to milk, substitute these ingredients when baking bread:

Almond and other nut milks
Apple juice
Fruit juice (if acidic, add 1 teaspoon of baking soda to offset the acidity)
Rice and other grain milks, amasake
Soymilk
Vegetable juice
Water

Pumpkin Poppyseed Bread

Milk-free, lactose-free

LARGE

1⅛ cups vanilla soymilk	4 tablespoons poppyseeds
1 cup canned pumpkin	2 tablespoons vital gluten
¼ cup blackstrap molasses	1½ teaspoons pumpkin pie
2 cups whole wheat bread flour	spice
	1 teaspoon salt
2 cups unbleached bread flour	2 teaspoons yeast

A light-rising loaf. Spicy and crunchy, it makes a great snack bread.

MEDIUM

¾ cup vanilla soymilk	3 tablespoons poppyseeds
¾ cup canned pumpkin	1½ tablespoons vital gluten

3 tablespoons blackstrap
  molasses
1½ cups whole wheat
  bread flour
1½ cups unbleached bread
  flour

1 teaspoon pumpkin pie
  spice
¾ teaspoon salt
1½ teaspoons yeast

SMALL

½ cup vanilla soymilk
½ cup canned pumpkin
2 tablespoons blackstrap
  molasses
1 cup whole wheat bread
  flour
1 cup unbleached bread
  flour

2 tablespoons poppyseeds
1 tablespoon vital gluten
¾ teaspoon pumpkin pie
  spice
½ teaspoon salt
1 teaspoon yeast

Nutrition Facts (based on medium-size loaf)

Serving Size 3.047 ounces (86.37g)
Servings Per Container   10

Amount Per Serving

Calories 180   Calories from Fat 21

	% *Daily Value**
Total Fat 2g	3%
Saturated Fat 0g	0%
Cholesterol 0mg	0%
Sodium 177mg	0%
Total Carbohydrate 34g	11%
Dietary Fiber 2g	8%
Sugars 3g	
Protein 8g	

Vitamin A 44%		Vitamin C	1%
Calcium 11%		Iron	17%

*Percent Daily Values are based on a 2,000 calorie diet. Your daily values may be higher or lower depending on your calorie needs.

Chick-Pea and Onion Bread

Milk-free, lactose-free

LARGE

1½ cups soymilk
1 tablespoon honey
2 cups unbleached bread
  flour
1 cup garbanzo bean flour
1 cup whole wheat bread
  flour

¼ cup dehydrated onion
  flakes
2 tablespoons vital gluten
1 teaspoon salt
2½ teaspoons yeast

A high-rising, light loaf that is great when topped with bean spreads or soy cheese.

Nutrition Facts (based on medium-size loaf)

Serving Size 2.920 ounces (82.78g)

Servings Per Container   10

Amount Per Serving

Calories 158   Calories from Fat 14

	% *Daily Value**
Total Fat 2g	3%
Saturated Fat 0g	0%
Cholesterol 0mg	0%
Sodium 181mg	0%
Total Carbohydrate 30g	10%
Dietary Fiber 1g	4%
Sugars 1g	
Protein 7g	

Vitamin A	7%	Vitamin C	2%
Calcium	5%	Iron	9%

---

*Percent Daily Values are based on a 2,000 calorie diet. Your daily values may be higher or lower depending on your calorie needs.

MEDIUM

1 cup soymilk
¾ tablespoon honey
1½ cups unbleached bread
   flour
¾ cup garbanzo bean flour
¾ cup whole wheat bread
   flour

1½ tablespoons vital gluten
3 tablespoons dehydrated
   onion flakes
¾ teaspoon salt
1½ teaspoons yeast

SMALL

¾ cup soymilk
½ tablespoon honey
1 cup unbleached bread
   flour
½ cup garbanzo bean flour
½ cup whole wheat bread
   flour

1 tablespoon vital gluten
2 tablespoons dehydrated
   onion flakes
½ teaspoon salt
1 teaspoon yeast

Spelt Bread

Cow's milk–free, high-fiber

LARGE

1½ cups goat's milk
2 tablespoons blackstrap
   molasses
2 cups spelt
2 cups whole wheat bread
   flour

3 tablespoons vital gluten
1 teaspoon salt
2 teaspoons yeast

If you are allergic to milk, you may be able to tolerate goat's milk. Buy pasteurized goat's milk at health-food stores. The cream in the goat's milk makes this a soft, light bread that rises well.

MEDIUM

1⅛ cups goat's milk
1½ tablespoons blackstrap
 molasses
1½ cups spelt
1½ cups whole wheat
 bread flour

2 tablespoons vital gluten
¾ teaspoon salt
1½ teaspoons yeast

SMALL

¾ cup goat's milk
1 tablespoon blackstrap
 molasses
1 cup spelt
1 cup whole wheat bread
 flour

1½ tablespoons vital gluten
½ teaspoon salt
1 teaspoon yeast

Nutrition Facts (based on medium-size loaf)

Serving Size 2.484 ounces (70.41g)
Servings Per Container   10

Amount Per Serving

Calories 155   Calories from Fat 19

	% *Daily Value**
Total Fat 2g	3%
Saturated Fat 1g	5%
Cholesterol 3mg	1%
Sodium 178mg	0%
Total Carbohydrate 29g	10%
Dietary Fiber 3g	12%
Sugars 2g	
Protein 9g	

Vitamin A	1%	Vitamin C	0%
Calcium	6%	Iron	12%

*Percent Daily Values are based on a 2,000 calorie diet. Your daily values may be higher or lower depending on your calorie needs.

Peanut Butter and Honey Bread

Milk-free, lactose-free, high-protein, high-fiber

LARGE

1¾ cups water
4 tablespoons honey
½ cup peanut butter
½ cup thick rolled oats

4 cups whole wheat bread
  flour
1 teaspoon salt
4 teaspoons yeast

The peanut butter makes this a very tender "buttery" loaf. Spread slices with jam for a special treat.

Nutrition Facts (based on medium-size loaf)

Serving Size 3.142 ounces (89.06g)

Servings Per Container   10

Amount Per Serving

Calories 210   Calories from Fat 52

	% *Daily Value**
Total Fat 6g	9%
Saturated Fat 1g	5%
Cholesterol 0mg	0%
Sodium 220mg	0%
Total Carbohydrate 34g	11%
Dietary Fiber 3g	12%
Sugars 6g	
Protein 9g	

Vitamin A 0%	Vitamin C 0%
Calcium 1%	Iron 10%

---

*Percent Daily Values are based on a 2,000 calorie diet. Your daily values may be higher or lower depending on your calorie needs.

MEDIUM

1⅜ cups water	3 cups whole wheat bread
3 tablespoons honey	flour
⅜ cup peanut butter	¾ teaspoon salt
⅜ cup thick rolled oats	3 teaspoons yeast

SMALL

⅞ cup water	2 cups whole wheat bread
2 tablespoons honey	flour
¼ cup peanut butter	½ teaspoon salt
¼ cup thick rolled oats	2 teaspoons yeast

Triticale Soy Bread

Milk-free, lactose-free, high-protein, low-fat

LARGE

1⅓ cups nonfat soymilk	1 cup rolled triticale
½ cup applesauce	⅓ cup soy flour
¼ cup molasses	3 tablespoons vital gluten
3 cups whole wheat bread	1 teaspoon salt
flour	2½ teaspoons yeast

A medium-rising, rich, chewy bread. It is a good sandwich bread for the teens in your family because of its calcium, iron, and protein content.

MEDIUM

1 cup nonfat soymilk	¾ cup rolled triticale
⅓ cup applesauce	¼ cup soy flour
3 tablespoons molasses	2½ tablespoons vital gluten
2¼ cups whole wheat	¾ teaspoon salt
bread flour	2 teaspoons yeast

SMALL

⅔ cup nonfat soymilk
¼ cup applesauce
⅛ cup molasses
1½ cups whole wheat
   bread flour

½ cup rolled triticale
⅛ cup soy flour
1½ tablespoons vital gluten
½ teaspoon salt
1½ teaspoons yeast

Nutrition Facts (based on medium-size loaf)

Serving Size 2.870 ounces (81.37g)

Servings Per Container   10

Amount Per Serving

Calories 157   Calories from Fat 15

	% *Daily Value**
Total Fat 2g	3%
Saturated Fat 0g	0%
Cholesterol 0mg	0%
Sodium 180mg	0%
Total Carbohydrate 32g	11%
Dietary Fiber 2g	8%
Sugars 3g	
Protein 8g	

Vitamin A	5%	Vitamin C	1%
Calcium	9%	Iron	15%

---

*Percent Daily Values are based on a 2,000 calorie diet. Your daily values may be higher or lower depending on your calorie needs.

Barley Flaxseed Bread

Milk-free, lactose-free, high-protein, low-fat, high-fiber

LARGE

1¾ cups apple juice	4 tablespoons vital gluten
½ cup applesauce	4 tablespoons flaxseeds
3 cups whole wheat bread	1 teaspoon salt
flour	2 teaspoons yeast
1½ cups rolled barley	

The apple juice gives this bread a nice rise and flavor. It is moist and sweet without a pronounced apple flavor.

Nutrition Facts (based on medium-size loaf)

Serving Size 3.073 ounces (87.12g)

Servings Per Container   10

Amount Per Serving

Calories 165   Calories from Fat 14

	% *Daily Value**
Total Fat 2g	3%
Saturated Fat 0g	0%
Cholesterol 0mg	0%
Sodium 165mg	0%
Total Carbohydrate 34g	11%
Dietary Fiber 4g	16%
Sugars 0g	
Protein 8g	

Vitamin A 0%	Vitamin C 24%
Calcium 2%	Iron 11%

---

*Percent Daily Values are based on a 2,000 calorie diet. Your daily values may be higher or lower depending on your calorie needs.

MEDIUM

1⅓ cups apple juice
⅓ cup applesauce
2¼ cups whole wheat
    bread flour
1⅛ cups rolled barley

3 tablespoons vital gluten
3 tablespoons flaxseeds
¾ teaspoon salt
1½ teaspoons yeast

SMALL

⅞ cup apple juice
¼ cup applesauce
1½ cups whole wheat
    bread flour
¾ cup rolled barley

2 tablespoons vital gluten
2 tablespoons flaxseeds
½ teaspoon salt
1 teaspoon yeast

Carrot Apple Bread

Milk-free, lactose-free, high-fiber

LARGE

1⅓ cups soymilk
½ cup applesauce
½ cup grated carrot
½ cup chopped apples
2 cups whole wheat bread
    flour
2 cups unbleached bread
    flour

¼ cup date sugar
2 tablespoons vital gluten
1 teaspoon salt
2½ teaspoons yeast

This bread is a real lunch in a loaf. It contains legumes, vegetables, fruit, and grains. Add the carrot and apples with the liquid ingredients. The apples and carrots will add water to the dough as they cook, so be careful not too add too much soymilk.

MEDIUM

1 cup soymilk
⅓ cup applesauce
⅓ cup grated carrot
⅓ cup chopped apples
1½ cups whole wheat
    bread flour

1½ cups unbleached bread
    flour
3 tablespoons date sugar
1½ tablespoons vital gluten
¾ teaspoon salt
2 teaspoons yeast

SMALL

⅔ cup soymilk
¼ cup applesauce
¼ cup grated carrot
¼ cup chopped apples

1 cup unbleached bread
    flour
2 tablespoons date sugar
1 tablespoon vital gluten

Nutrition Facts (based on medium-size loaf)

Serving Size 2.971 ounces (84.24g)
Servings Per Container   10

Amount Per Serving

Calories 167   Calories from Fat 11

	% Daily Value*
Total Fat 1g	2%
Saturated Fat 0g	0%
Cholesterol 0mg	0%
Sodium 175mg	0%
Total Carbohydrate 34g	11%
Dietary Fiber 2g	8%
Sugars 3g	
Protein 7g	

Vitamin A 15%	Vitamin C 1%
Calcium 4%	Iron 11%

---

*Percent Daily Values are based on a 2,000 calorie diet. Your daily values may be higher or lower depending on your calorie needs.

1 cup whole wheat bread   ½ teaspoon salt
flour   1½ teaspoons yeast

Prune Oat Bread

Milk-free, lactose-free, high-protein, high-fiber, low-fat

LARGE

1¾ cups water
1 cup dried, pitted prunes
4 cups whole wheat bread
flour
¾ cup thick rolled oats

4 tablespoons vital gluten
2 tablespoons date sugar
1 teaspoon salt
2½ teaspoons yeast

Nutrition Facts (based on medium-size loaf)

Serving Size 3.089 ounces (87.56g)

Servings Per Container   10

Amount Per Serving

Calories 170   Calories from Fat 10

	% *Daily Value**
Total Fat 1g	2%
Saturated Fat 0g	0%
Cholesterol 0mg	0%
Sodium 164mg	0%
Total Carbohydrate 36g	12%
Dietary Fiber 3g	12%
Sugars 6g	
Protein 9g	

Vitamin A 2%	Vitamin C 0%
Calcium 2%	Iron 11%

*Percent Daily Values are based on a 2,000 calorie diet. Your daily values may be higher or lower depending on your calorie needs.

This bread seldom even makes it to the cutting board. It's a medium-rising, sweet bread that disappears at our house before it has a chance to cool.

MEDIUM

1¼ cups water
¾ cup dried, pitted prunes
3 cups whole wheat bread
    flour
½ cup thick rolled oats

3 tablespoons vital gluten
1½ tablespoons date sugar
¾ teaspoon salt
2 teaspoons yeast

SMALL

⅞ cup water
½ cup dried, pitted prunes
2 cups whole wheat bread
    flour
⅜ cup thick rolled oats

2 tablespoons vital gluten
1 tablespoon date sugar
½ teaspoon salt
1½ teaspoons yeast

Banana Muesli Bread

Milk-free, lactose-free, low-fat, high-fiber

LARGE

1½ cups vanilla soymilk
¾ cup mashed ripe banana
2 tablespoons blackstrap
    molasses
3 cups whole wheat bread
    flour

2 cups muesli
4 tablespoons vital gluten
1 teaspoon salt
2½ teaspoons yeast

A good breakfast bread for those who don't have time to eat breakfast. Two slices on the way to work will give you a third of the iron and fiber you need for the day, all with only 2 grams of fat.

Medium

1⅛ cups vanilla soymilk
½ cup mashed ripe banana
1½ tablespoons blackstrap
   molasses
2¼ cups whole wheat
   bread flour

1½ cups muesli
3 tablespoons vital gluten
¾ teaspoon salt
2 teaspoons yeast

Small

¾ cup vanilla soymilk
⅓ cup mashed ripe banana

1 cup muesli
2 tablespoons vital gluten

Nutrition Facts (based on medium-size loaf)

Serving Size 3.124 ounces (88.56g)
Servings Per Container   10

Amount Per Serving

Calories 177   Calories from Fat 12

	% *Daily Value**
Total Fat 1g	2%
Saturated Fat 0g	0%
Cholesterol 0mg	0%
Sodium 203mg	0%
Total Carbohydrate 38g	13%
Dietary Fiber 3g	12%
Sugars 5g	
Protein 9g	

Vitamin A 0%	Vitamin C 2%
Calcium 4%	Iron 14%

*Percent Daily Values are based on a 2,000 calorie diet. Your daily values may be higher or lower depending on your calorie needs.

1 tablespoon blackstrap
   molasses
1½ cups whole wheat
   bread flour

½ teaspoon salt
1½ teaspoons yeast

Tomato Potato Bread

Milk-free, lactose-free, low-fat

LARGE

1⅓ cups tomato juice
3 tablespoons extra virgin
   olive oil
2 cups whole wheat bread
   flour
1 cup potato starch flour
1½ cups unbleached bread
   flour

3 tablespoons vital gluten
3 tablespoons dried parsley
1 teaspoon salt (not
   needed if tomato juice
   contains salt)
2 teaspoons yeast

A light orange loaf with specks of green. Serve it with soup or as an open-faced sandwich with soy cheese and tomatoes.

MEDIUM

1 cup tomato juice
2½ tablespoons extra virgin
   olive oil
1½ cups whole wheat
   bread flour
¾ cup potato starch flour
1⅛ cups unbleached bread
   flour

2 tablespoons vital gluten
2 tablespoons dried parsley
¾ teaspoon salt (not
   needed if tomato juice
   contains salt)
1½ teaspoons yeast

SMALL

⅔ cup tomato juice

1½ tablespoons extra virgin olive oil

1 cup whole wheat bread flour

½ cup potato starch flour

¾ cup unbleached bread flour

1½ tablespoons vital gluten

1½ tablespoons dried parsley

½ teaspoon salt (not needed if tomato juice contains salt)

1 teaspoon yeast

Nutrition Facts (based on medium-size loaf)

Serving Size 2.862 ounces (81.14g)

Servings Per Container   10

Amount Per Serving

Calories 192　　　　Calories from Fat 36

% *Daily Value**

Total Fat 4g	6%
Saturated Fat 1g	5%
Cholesterol 0mg	0%
Sodium 116mg	0%
Total Carbohydrate 35g	12%
Dietary Fiber 2g	8%
Sugars 1g	
Protein 6g	

Vitamin A	1%	Vitamin C	7%
Calcium	1%	Iron	11%

*Percent Daily Values are based on a 2,000 calorie diet. Your daily values may be higher or lower depending on your calorie needs.

CHAPTER 14

Wheat-Free Breads

Recommended for: wheat allergy

Wheat is one of the oldest cultivated food plants and one of the most abundant food crops. Of the cereal flours, it is the highest in gluten and produces the lighest bread. Multigrain store-bought breads are made primarily with wheat flour to give them a light texture.

Wheat Allergy

Wheat contains at least four different proteins that can cause allergic reactions: gliadin, globulin, glutenin, and albumin. Wheat allergies can come from eating the grain or from inhaling fine wheat flour particles (the cause of "baker's asthma"). Since wheat is a major food product in this country, locating wheat-free products can be difficult. Remember always to read food labels. Wheat can turn up in a number of ingredients you would not expect it to be in.

Substitutions for Wheat

Fortunately, the individual with a wheat allergy can safely eat a variety of other flours. Spelt is a grain suitable for individuals with wheat alleries that is also high in gluten. It can be supplemented with barley, rye, and oats, which contain small amounts of gluten to give a light, medium-rising loaf.

If you are allergic to wheat, avoid these bread ingredients:

Farina
Flour (enriched or unbleached)
Gluten, high-gluten flour, or vital gluten
Graham flour
Malted cereal syrup
Modified food starch
Triticale (a hybrid of wheat and rye)
Wheat bran
Wheat flour
Wheat germ
Wheat starch
Whole wheat flour

Here are some substitutes to use for wheat in bread:

Amaranth
Barley flour
Corn meal
Garbanzo bean flour
Millet
Oat flour
Potato starch flour
Quinoa
Rice bran
Rice flour
Rice polish
Rye flour
Soy flour
Spelt
Teff

Guidelines for Baking Wheat-Free Breads

1. Do not buy ingredients from open bulk containers. They may be contaminated with wheat flour.
2. Products that are marked gluten-free can also be safely used by those with wheat allergies.
3. A mixture of two or three flours will give better results than use of a single flour.
4. For higher rising loaves, use spelt flour as the base for your recipes. Combine it with smaller amounts of flours that have less gluten.
5. For a milder tasting bread, add light flours such as tapioca flour and potato starch flour to the recipe.

Spelt Molasses Bread

Wheat-free, lactose-free

LARGE

1½ cups soymilk	4 tablespoons molasses
2 tablespoons canola oil	3½ teaspoons xanthan gum
1½ cups brown rice flour	4 teaspoons yeast
2½ cups spelt flour	1½ teaspoons salt

Spelt gives this loaf a lovely high rise. It is slighty sweet and goes well with nut butters.

MEDIUM

1⅛ cups soymilk	3 tablespoons molasses
1½ tablespoons canola oil	2 teaspoons xanthan gum
1 cup brown rice flour	3 teaspoons yeast
2 cups spelt flour	1 teaspoon salt

SMALL

¾ cup soymilk   2 tablespoons molasses
1 tablespoon canola oil   1½ teaspoons xanthan gum
¾ cup brown rice flour   2½ teaspoons yeast
1¼ cups spelt flour   ¾ teaspoon salt

Nutrition Facts (based on medium-size loaf)

Serving Size 2.834 ounces (80.34g)
Servings Per Container   10

Amount Per Serving

Calories 200   Calories from Fat 35

                                    % *Daily Value**

Total Fat 4g   6%
  Saturated Fat 0g   0%
Cholesterol 0mg   0%
Sodium 235mg   0%
Total Carbohydrate 36g   12%
  Dietary Fiber 4g   16%
  Sugars 0g
Protein 5g

Vitamin A   5%   Vitamin C   0%
Calcium   8%   Iron   15%

---

*Percent Daily Values are based on a 2,000 calorie diet. Your daily values may be higher or lower depending on your calorie needs.

Spelt Raisin Bread

Wheat-free, lactose-free, high-protein, high-fiber

LARGE

1½ cups nonfat soymilk or   1½ tablespoons canola oil
  rice milk   4 cups spelt flour
4 eggs   1½ teaspoons salt
⅓ cup maple syrup   4 teaspoons yeast

If your machine has a raisin bread cycle, add this at the beep; otherwise, add after first knead:

¾ cup raisins

MEDIUM

1⅛ cups nonfat soymilk or rice milk	1 tablespoon canola oil
	3 cups spelt flour
3 eggs	1 teaspoon salt
¼ cup maple syrup	3 teaspoons yeast

If your machine has a raisin bread cycle, add this at the beep; otherwise, add after first knead:

½ cup raisins

Nutrition Facts (based on medium-size loaf)

Serving Size 3.401 ounces (96.42g)

Servings Per Container   10

Amount Per Serving

Calories 234   Calories from Fat 42

	% *Daily Value**
Total Fat 5g	8%
Saturated Fat 1g	5%
Cholesterol 64mg	21%
Sodium 248mg	0%
Total Carbohydrate 40g	13%
Dietary Fiber 5g	20%
Sugars 5g	
Protein 8g	

Vitamin A	8%	Vitamin C	0%
Calcium	5%	Iron	13%

*Percent Daily Values are based on a 2,000 calorie diet. Your daily values may be higher or lower depending on your calorie needs.

SMALL

¾ cup nonfat soymilk or
  rice milk
2 eggs
⅕ cup maple syrup

¾ tablespoon canola oil
2 cups spelt flour
¾ teaspoon salt
2½ teaspoons yeast

If your machine has a raisin bread cycle, add this at the beep;
otherwise, add after first knead:

⅓ cup raisins

Amaranth Egg Bread

Wheat-free, lactose-free, high-protein, high-fiber

LARGE

2 cups nonfat soymilk or
  rice milk
4 eggs
2 cups spelt flour
1 cup amaranth flour
1 cup rice polish

½ cup millet seeds
½ cup toasted sesame
  seeds
4 tablespoons honey
2 teaspoons salt
5 teaspoons yeast

Two slices of this bread will provide 22 grams of protein, half
of the iron, a fifth of the calcium, and a third of the fiber that
you need for the day. A few slices make a nutritious meal all by
themselves.

MEDIUM

1½ cups nonfat soymilk or
  rice milk
3 eggs
1½ cups spelt flour
¾ cup amaranth flour
¾ cup rice polish

⅜ cup millet seeds
⅜ cup toasted sesame
  seeds
3 tablespoons honey
1½ teaspoons salt
3½ teaspoons yeast

SMALL

1 cup nonfat soymilk or
  rice milk
2 eggs
1 cup spelt flour
½ cup amaranth flour
½ cup rice polish

¼ cup millet seeds
¼ cup toasted sesame
  seeds
2 tablespoons honey
1 teaspoon salt
2½ teaspoons yeast

Nutrition Facts (based on medium-size loaf)

Serving Size 3.910 ounces (110.9g)
Servings Per Container   10

Amount Per Serving

Calories 273   Calories from Fat 64

	% Daily Value*
Total Fat 7g	11%
Saturated Fat 2g	10%
Cholesterol 64mg	21%
Sodium 376mg	0%
Total Carbohydrate 45g	15%
Dietary Fiber 5g	20%
Sugars 5g	
Protein 11g	

Vitamin A 2%	Vitamin C 1%
Calcium 10%	Iron 26%

*Percent Daily Values are based on a 2,000 calorie diet. Your daily values may be higher or lower depending on your calorie needs.

Banana Walnut Bread

Wheat-free, lactose-free, high-protein

LARGE

½ cup soymilk
3 ripe medium bananas,
    mashed
1½ cups oat flour
1½ cups brown rice flour
1½ cups potato starch flour
1 cup thick rolled oats

1 cup chopped walnuts
½ cup date sugar
6 teaspoons xanthan gum
1½ teaspoons salt
1½ teaspoons cinnamon
4½ teaspoons yeast

A sensory delight! This makes a low-rising, chewy, sweet loaf.

Nutrition Facts (based on medium-size loaf)

Serving Size 3.828 ounces (108.5g)

Servings Per Container   10

Amount Per Serving

Calories 273   Calories from Fat 61

	% Daily Value*
Total Fat 7g	11%
Saturated Fat 1g	5%
Cholesterol 0mg	0%
Sodium 229mg	0%
Total Carbohydrate 49g	16%
Dietary Fiber 3g	12%
Sugars 8g	
Protein 7g	

Vitamin A	0%	Vitamin C	4%
Calcium	3%	Iron	12%

*Percent Daily Values are based on a 2,000 calorie diet. Your daily values may be higher or lower depending on your calorie needs.

MEDIUM

⅓ cup soymilk
2 ripe medium bananas,
 mashed
1 cup oat flour
1 cup brown rice flour
1 cup potato starch flour
¾ cup thick rolled oats

¾ cup chopped walnuts
⅜ cup date sugar
4½ teaspoons xanthan gum
1 teaspoon salt
1 teaspoon cinnamon
3½ teaspoons yeast

SMALL

¼ cup soymilk
1½ ripe medium bananas,
 mashed
¾ cup oat flour
¾ cup brown rice flour
¾ cup potato starch flour
½ cup thick rolled oats

½ cup chopped walnuts
¼ cup date sugar
3 teaspoons xanthan gum
¾ teaspoon salt
¾ teaspoon cinnamon
3 teaspoons yeast

Herbal Spelt Bread

Wheat-free, high-protein, high-fiber

LARGE

1½ cups nonfat milk
4 eggs
4 cups spelt flour
4 teaspoons honey
1½ teaspoons salt

1½ tablespoons crushed
 coriander seeds
1½ tablespoons crushed
 anise seeds
4 teaspoons yeast

Light and airy because of the eggs. This bread is good source of protein for finicky eaters.

MEDIUM

1 cup nonfat milk
3 eggs
3 cups spelt flour
3 teaspoons honey
1 teaspoon salt

1 tablespoon crushed
  coriander seeds
1 tablespoon crushed anise
  seeds
3 teaspoons yeast

SMALL

¾ cup nonfat milk
2 eggs
2 cups spelt flour
2 teaspoons honey
¾ teaspoon salt

¾ tablespoon crushed
  coriander seeds
¾ tablespoon crushed anise
  seeds
2 teaspoons yeast

Nutrition Facts (based on medium-size loaf)

Serving Size 2.773 ounces (78.61g)
Servings Per Container   10

Amount Per Serving

Calories 190   Calories from Fat 26

	% *Daily Value**
Total Fat 3g	5%
Saturated Fat 1g	5%
Cholesterol 64mg	21%
Sodium 255mg	0%
Total Carbohydrate 33g	11%
Dietary Fiber 5g	20%
Sugars 2g	
Protein 8g	

Vitamin A	3%	Vitamin C	0%
Calcium	2%	Iron	13%

*Percent Daily Values are based on a 2,000 calorie diet. Your daily values may be higher or lower depending on your calorie needs.

Mexican Corn Bread

Wheat-free, lactose-free, high-protein, high-fiber

LARGE

1½ cups soymilk	4 tablespoons honey
½ cup olive oil	⅙ teaspoon cayenne
4 eggs	pepper
2 cups spelt flour	1 teaspoon cumin
2 cups cornmeal	2½ teaspoons salt
1 cup corn flour (polenta)	4 teaspoons yeast

If your machine has a raisin bread cycle, add this at the beep; otherwise, add after second knead:

4 tablespoons chopped
   green chilies

A nutritious high-fiber bread. The chilies make this loaf spectacular!

MEDIUM

1 cup soymilk	3 tablespoons honey
⅓ cup olive oil	⅛ teaspoon cayenne
3 eggs	pepper
1½ cups spelt flour	¾ teaspoon cumin
1½ cups cornmeal	2 teaspoons salt
¾ cup corn flour (polenta)	3 teaspoons yeast

If your machine has a raisin bread cycle, add this at the beep; otherwise, add after second knead:

3 tablespoons chopped
   green chilies

SMALL

¾ cup soymilk   2 tablespoons honey
¼ cup olive oil   1 pinch cayenne pepper
2 eggs   ½ teaspoon cumin
1 cup spelt flour   1½ teaspoons salt
1 cup cornmeal   2 teaspoons yeast
½ cup corn flour (polenta)

If your machine has a raisin bread cycle, add this at the beep;
otherwise, add after second knead:

2 tablespoons chopped
    green chilies

Nutrition Facts (based on medium-
size loaf)
Serving Size 3.590 ounces (101.8g)
Servings Per Container   10

Amount Per Serving
Calories 294   Calories from Fat 93

                              % *Daily Value**
Total Fat 10g   15%
   Saturated Fat 2g   10%
Cholesterol 64mg   21%
Sodium 478mg   0%
Total Carbohydrate 44g   15%
   Dietary Fiber 7g   28%
   Sugars 5g
Protein 8g

Vitamin A   4%   Vitamin C   7%
Calcium   2%   Iron   13%

---

*Percent Daily Values are based on a 2,000
calorie diet. Your daily values may be higher
or lower depending on your calorie needs.

Italian Herb Bread

Wheat-free, high-fiber

LARGE

2 cups water
4 tablespoons extra virgin
 olive oil
1 cup fresh basil or 4
 tablespoons dried basil
4 tablespoons grated
 parmesan cheese

4 tablespoons chopped
 fresh garlic
4 cups spelt flour
½ cup rice polish
2 tablespoons date sugar
½ teaspoon salt
4 teaspoons yeast

This fragrant loaf is a must for garlic lovers. Use fresh basil
when you can and serve this bread with wheat-free pasta.

MEDIUM

1½ cups water
3 tablespoons olive oil
¾ cup fresh basil or 3
 tablespoons dried basil
3 tablespoons grated
 parmesan cheese
3 tablespoons chopped
 fresh garlic

3 cups spelt flour
⅜ cup rice polish
1½ tablespoons date sugar
¼ teaspoon salt
3 teaspoons yeast

SMALL

1 cup water
2 tablespoons olive oil
½ cup fresh basil or 2
 tablespoons dried basil
2 tablespoons grated
 parmesan cheese
2 tablespoons chopped
 fresh garlic

2 cups spelt flour
¼ cup rice polish
1 tablespoon date sugar
⅛ teaspoon salt
2½ teaspoons yeast

Nutrition Facts (based on medium-size loaf)
Serving Size 3.045 ounces (86.33g)
Servings Per Container   10

Amount Per Serving
Calories 204   Calories from Fat 57

	% *Daily Value**
Total Fat 6g	9%
Saturated Fat 1g	5%
Cholesterol 1mg	0%
Sodium 198mg	0%
Total Carbohydrate 31g	10%
Dietary Fiber 5g	20%
Sugars 1g	
Protein 7g	

Vitamin A	1%	Vitamin C	1%
Calcium	5%	Iron	15%

*Percent Daily Values are based on a 2,000 calorie diet. Your daily values may be higher or lower depending on your calorie needs.

Zucchini Carrot Bread

Wheat-free, high-protein, high-fiber

LARGE

1½ cups shredded zucchini
1½ cups shredded carrot
1 cup nonfat milk
4 eggs
5 cups spelt flour
¾ cup date sugar

2 teaspoons cinnamon
1 teaspoon salt
1 teaspoon nutmeg
⅓ teaspoon cloves
4 teaspoons yeast

Don't know what to do with all that zucchini in your garden?
Put it in your bread, and the kids will never find it! This is a
wonderfully easy way to sneak vegies into your offspring.

MEDIUM

1 cup shredded zucchini
1 cup shredded carrot
¾ cup nonfat milk
3 eggs
3¾ cups spelt flour
½ cup date sugar

1½ teaspoons cinnamon
¾ teaspoon salt
¾ teaspoon nutmeg
¼ teaspoon cloves
3 teaspoons yeast

Nutrition Facts (based on medium-size loaf)

Serving Size 3.998 ounces (113.3g)
Servings Per Container   10

Amount Per Serving

Calories 238   Calories from Fat 29

% *Daily Value**

Total Fat 3g	5%
Saturated Fat 1g	5%
Cholesterol 64mg	21%
Sodium 194mg	0%
Total Carbohydrate 43g	14%
Dietary Fiber 8g	32%
Sugars 7g	
Protein 9g	

Vitamin A	35%	Vitamin C	4%
Calcium	4%	Iron	15%

*Percent Daily Values are based on a 2,000 calorie diet. Your daily values may be higher or lower depending on your calorie needs.

SMALL

¾ cup shredded zucchini
¾ cup shredded carrot
½ cup nonfat milk
2 eggs
2½ cups spelt flour
¼ cup date sugar

1 teaspoon cinnamon
½ teaspoon salt
½ teaspoon nutmeg
⅛ teaspoon cloves
2 teaspoons yeast

Banana Rice Bread

Wheat-free, gluten-free, lactose-free, milk-free

LARGE

2 cups plain soymilk
1½ cups mashed banana
3 eggs
3 cups brown rice flour
¾ cup garbanzo bean flour
¾ cup rice polish

⅓ cup date sugar
6 teaspoons xanthan gum
3 tablespoons flaxseeds
1½ teaspoons salt
4½ teaspoons yeast

A sweet, medium-rising loaf that is also suitable for individuals who are gluten intolerant.

MEDIUM

1½ cups plain soymilk
1 cup mashed banana
2 eggs
2¼ cups brown rice flour
½ cup garbanzo bean flour
½ cup rice polish

¼ cup date sugar
4½ teaspoons xanthan gum
2 tablespoons flaxseeds
1 teaspoon salt
3½ teaspoons yeast

SMALL

1 cup plain soymilk
¾ cup mashed banana
1 egg plus 1 egg white

2½ tablespoons date sugar
3 teaspoons xanthan gum
1½ tablespoons flaxseeds

1½ cups brown rice flour
⅓ cup garbanzo bean flour
⅓ cup rice polish

¾ teaspoon salt
2½ teaspoons yeast

Nutrition Facts (based on medium-size loaf)

Serving Size 4.559 ounces (129.2g)

Servings Per Container   10

Amount Per Serving

Calories 224   Calories from Fat 37

	% *Daily Value**
Total Fat 4g	6%
Saturated Fat 1g	5%
Cholesterol 43mg	14%
Sodium 249mg	0%
Total Carbohydrate 42g	14%
Dietary Fiber 3g	12%
Sugars 3g	
Protein 7g	

Vitamin A	9%	Vitamin C	3%
Calcium	6%	Iron	13%

*Percent Daily Values are based on a 2,000 calorie diet. Your daily values may be higher or lower depending on your calorie needs.

Vanilla Spelt Bread

Wheat-free, lactose-free, milk-free, high-protein

LARGE

1½ cups nonfat soymilk or
   rice milk
5 eggs plus 1 egg white
2 teaspoons vanilla extract

4 cups spelt flour
4 tablespoons date sugar
4 teaspoons yeast
2 teaspoons salt

This recipe makes a fluffy, aromatic loaf that is hard to resist.

MEDIUM

1 cup nonfat soymilk or rice milk	3 cups spelt flour
4 eggs	3 tablespoons date sugar
1½ teaspoons vanilla extract	3 teaspoons yeast
	1½ teaspoons salt

SMALL

¾ cup nonfat soymilk or rice milk	2 cups spelt flour
2 eggs plus 1 egg white	2 tablespoons date sugar
1 teaspoon vanilla extract	2 teaspoons yeast
	1 teaspoon salt

Nutrition Facts (based on medium-size loaf)

Serving Size 2.988 ounces (84.70g)

Servings Per Container   10

Amount Per Serving

Calories 198   Calories from Fat 29

	% *Daily Value**
Total Fat 3g	5%
Saturated Fat 1g	5%
Cholesterol 85mg	28%
Sodium 367mg	0%
Total Carbohydrate 33g	11%
Dietary Fiber 5g	20%
Sugars 2g	
Protein 9g	

Vitamin A	3%	Vitamin C	0%
Calcium	2%	Iron	11%

---

*Percent Daily Values are based on a 2,000 calorie diet. Your daily values may be higher or lower depending on your calorie needs.

Glossary

Dairy Products

Dairy products are not necessary for bread baking, but the addition of one or more of the following ingredients can make a dramatic difference in the flavor and texture of a loaf of bread.

Butter   Butter adds flavor and a satisfying mouth feel to bread. It also makes bread softer but is a concentrated source of saturated fat and cholesterol. There are many nutritious alternatives to butter for bread recipes.

Buttermilk   Buttermilk is produced by adding a bacterial culture (as in yogurt), called lactobacilli, to either low-fat or skim milk. The result is a low-fat, creamy ingredient that makes a light, high-rising, and tender bread loaf. It can be substituted in recipes by adding two tablespoons of yogurt or sour cream and one tablespoon of vinegar or lemon juice to a cup and adding milk to equal one cup.

Cottage cheese   Cottage cheese is white and has a soft curd and mild, milky flavor. Add to sweet or savory recipes for a tender and moist loaf without adding a lot of fat.

Milk   Milk can be used in place of water in almost all recipes. It encourages a softer crust and more tender crumb. The richer the milk, the softer the crumb. There are many alternatives to dairy (cow's) milk. One is soymilk, which comes in plain, vanilla, carob, or cocoa flavor and has the options of low-fat and whole-fat. The latest option is nutrient-fortified soymilk, which has a nutritional composition similar to that of cow's milk. The advantages of soymilk include an alternative for those with milk allergies and a no-cholesterol option. Also available are nut milks, such as almond milk, which is high in protein, calcium, iron, magnesium, phosphorus, and potassium. Rice milk is another sweet and creamy alternative milk and is available in health-food stores.

Parmesan cheese   Parmesan cheese, which is used either grated, powdered, or shredded, can be added to herb breads for rich and chewy loaves. It is usually very high in sodium, so cut back to one-eighth teaspoon of salt when using parmesan.

Ricotta cheese   Ricotta cheese is a healthful low-fat alternative to butter for bread machine baking. It is a soft, moist, and slightly sweet cheese. Because whey is used, ricotta has less fat and calories than cottage cheese yet is similar in most qualities. Dried ricotta can also be grated and added to recipes.

Yogurt   Yogurt is the perfect substitute for butter in almost all bread recipes. Use up to 1 cup per one-pound bread recipe and decrease the amount of liquid accordingly. For example, if you add one-quarter cup of yogurt to a recipe, subtract one-quarter cup of the water or other liquid normally called for in that recipe.

Flours

Flour is the base for all bread recipes. Choose high-quality, fresh grain or vegetable flours for best results and optimum nutrition. Store flours in airtight containers in a cool, dry place for up to several months. For longer shelf life, store in the freezer.

Amaranth flour   Amaranth flour is a high-protein grain flour from Central America. It is an alternative whole grain flour for those with wheat allergies. This grain flour can be used as one-quarter of the total flour in a bread recipe to add protein and a sweet, nutty, mild flavor. Amaranth is a higher quality protein than almost all other grains because it is rich in all the essential amino acids, especially lysine, which is limited in many common grains.

Artichoke flour Artichoke flour is a vegetable flour rather than a grain flour. It is made from the Jerusalem artichoke (sun choke) and can be used as up to 10 percent of the total flour combination in a recipe. A few of its nutritional benefits are aiding blood sugar level maintenance and introducing healthful bacteria to the intestinal tract.

Barley flour Barley flour is a low-gluten grain flour that works like rye but is just a bit stickier. Using half rye flour and half whole wheat flour makes a light loaf that is milder tasting than 100 percent whole wheat. Adding barley flakes instead of barley flour will add texture as well as taste.

Buckwheat flour Buckwheat flour makes a heavy, high-protein bread. It is best when mixed with other flours. It is made of ground buckwheat groats (whole, unpolished, unfrosted buckwheat kernels). Light buckwheat flour is ground with very little hull, has a delicate flavor, and is light in color. Dark buckwheat flour is ground with the hull and has a strong flavor. The protein content is around 15 percent, the fat content is low, and it is a rich source of thiamin and niacin.

Bulgur Bulgur (or bulghur) is a parboiled (lightly cooked and parched) and cracked wheat product. It has a delicate nutty flavor. Because it has been precooked and lightly processed, this grain product takes only fifteen minutes in a bowl of hot water to be cooked enough to serve or mix into a recipe.

Corn flour Corn flour, or cornmeal, is a vegetable flour. When mixed with other flours, it gives bread a sweet flavor and rich gritty texture while adding protein. It is made from yellow, blue, or white corn kernels that have been finely ground. Blue corn has a considerably higher protein content. Cornmeal may be labeled "stone ground," which indicates a slightly coarser milling than regular cornmeal. Use it in combination with higher gluten flours for a crumbly textured bread. Whole ground cornmeal is rich in protein, carbohydrate, vitamin A, calcium, and vitamin E. Both yellow corn and white corn are ground and sold as cornmeal in most natural-foods stores.

Garbanzo flour Garbanzo flour is a bean flour made from the garbanzo bean, also known as the chick-pea. Garbanzo beans add a considerable amount of protein to bread and are widely available dried whole, fresh, canned, or packaged as flour. This flour is suitable for those with celiac disease.

Gluten flour   Gluten is the elastic plant protein present to some degree in almost all flours. It serves as a bread conditioner that stretches during the kneading cycle; it gives the dough a chewy, elastic quality and rising ability and holds it all together. White flours contains plenty of gluten, but some whole grain flours do not. Adding some high-gluten (white) flour or gluten extract (vital gluten) to a low-gluten flour recipe will make for better rising and texture. For those with allergies to wheat or a complete gluten intolerance, it is possible to use a combination of nongluten flours that produces beautiful loaves of bread. Vital gluten (gluten extract) is available in a powdered form wherever quality baking supplies are sold. It is commonly used to improve the rising ability of bread doughs. Gluten flour is used as an addition when baking with low-gluten flours. It is made by removing most of the starch from high-protein, hard-wheat flour, leaving a product high in gluten.

Kamut flour   Kamut flour is made from a revived ancient grain of Egypt. It has a rich flavor, high protein content, and significant amounts of magnesium and zinc. It has become widely used as an alternative to wheat, America's number one food allergen. Those with wheat sensitivities often find kamut to be a viable alternative to wheat.

Millet flour   Millet flour is made from the tiny, yellow, round millet grain kernels. A significant level of iron and well-balanced amino acids give millet high nutritional scores. It cannot be used alone but adds a slightly nutty flavor and crunchy texture to bread. Combine with whole wheat flour using two parts whole wheat flour to one part millet flour.

Oat flour   Oat flour gives a light, crumbly texture when mixed with whole wheat or corn flour. It is available in most health-food stores.

Quinoa flour   Quinoa flour is very low in gluten and rich in histadine and lysine, the limiting amino acids in other grains. Famed for its high protein and mineral content, it has an agreeable flavor and is found in most health-food stores. This is a suitable flour for those with wheat allergies.

Pumpernickel flour   Pumpernickel is a coarse grade of rye. Due to its high bran content, it makes a dense loaf. Pumpernickel flour can be purchased in specialty shops or through the mail. If pumpernickel is unavailable, rye can be substituted.

Rice flour   Rice flour is now available as brown rice flour, which has its germ and bran incorporated into the flour for higher nutritional quality. It is also available as white rice flour, rice meal, and sweet rice flour. Each of these gives bread a sweet flavor and silky quality. Rice products serve as a staple ingredient in gluten-free loaves for those with gluten intolerance.

Rye flour   Rye flour is another low-gluten flour. It looks a lot like whole wheat flour but gives a stickier and finer textured bread. For lighter bread, combine rye flour with whole wheat flour. From 20 to 30 percent of the flour content in bread can be rye; the rest should be a high-gluten flour to lighten and give rise to the bread. White rye is used in rye bread, and dark rye is used for pumpernickel.

Self-rising flour   Self-rising flour is a white wheat flour to which baking powder and sometimes salt have been added. It is generally made from bleached white flour. This product should not be used in bread machine baking.

Semolina flour   Semolina is a wheat generally used for pasta. Made from protein-rich durum wheat with only its bran removed, semolina flour is strong and rises well.

Soybean flour   Soybean flour adds sweetness and, like all bean flours, considerable protein content to a recipe. Its inherent fat content makes a crust that browns quickly and stays fresh longer. It is gluten-free; therefore, best results are achieved when it is used as no more than one-fifth of the flour mixture. This high-protein flour adds moisture to bread. Defatted soy flour is available but should be avoided, as it is treated with chemical solvents.

Spelt flour   Spelt flour has a high gluten content and makes light, high-rising loaves of bread. Spelt is biologically closely related to wheat, yet those with wheat allergies can often tolerate spelt. It is mild in flavor and has a very appealing taste.

Tapioca flour   Tapioca is derived from the root of the tropical plant known as manioc or cassava. Tapioca flour is a good alternative flour for those with celiac disease.

Teff flour   Teff is another of the ancient grains now sold in health-food stores and found at co-ops as a whole grain or flour. It has an earthy, nutty flavor that works well in breads. It is only remotely related to wheat and considered essentially gluten free. Teff is a staple alternative for those who have allergies to wheat. It contains 10 percent protein and 13.5 percent fiber.

Triticale flour   Triticale flour is milled from triticale, a hybrid grain of rye and wheat. It is best used as one-third of the flour mixture, with the other two-thirds from a high-gluten whole wheat flour.

Unbleached white flour Unbleached white flour is wheat flour that has been bleached naturally with aging rather than a chemical bleaching process. In all other aspects it is the same as white flour.

White flour White flour, or all-purpose flour, is high in gluten but lacks nutritional quality, as it has been highly processed. The vitamin-containing germ as well as the fibrous (bran) portion have been removed.

Whole wheat flour Whole wheat flour has the bran and germ intact but does not have the rising ability that white flour does. Therefore, using a combination of high-gluten and whole wheat flour will bring best rising results. For those who wish to use all whole grain flours in their baking for their nutritional quality, it is possible to enhance the rising ability of the dough by adding more yeast or vital gluten. See Chapter 6 and the basic breads Trouble-shooting Guide in Chapter 5 for more ideas. Purchase whole wheat bread flour (also referred to as graham flour, which is a coarse grind of whole wheat flour), not pastry flour. Germ (wheat germ) contains healthful fat-soluble vitamins such as vitamin E and B vitamins and also contains fiber.

Grains

There are many whole grains and whole grain products on the market. These products range from by-products of the milling process such as bran or germ to whole grain cereal mixes such as muesli or rolled oats. These products are rich in nutritional value from vitamins to fiber and have a vast culinary value in adding flavor and texture to bread.

Bran Bran is the fiber-containing part of the grain kernel. Wheat bran, rice bran, and oat bran can be found at most grocery stores. Bran contains many vitamins, trace minerals, and protein and is high in dietary fiber. Oat bran has received much attention for its soluble fiber content, which aids in lowering blood cholesterol. Adding up to several tablespoons of bran to each bread recipe minimally affects flavor and texture, yet adds significant amounts of healthy dietary fiber.

Cracked wheat Cracked wheat is coarsely ground, toasted whole wheat berries. It has a nutty flavor and crunchy texture. Couscous is refined cracked wheat which lacks bran and germ and has been parboiled before being crushed. Couscous cooks quickly, in about ten minutes, and can be added uncooked to bread recipes.

Endosperm The endosperm is the starchy center of the grain kernel, which is milled to make white flour.

Germ The germ is the part of a grain kernel that would germinate the plant and provide nutrients for it to grow. The germ generally contains concentrated amounts of B complex vitamins, vitamin E, calcium, iron, magnesium, and zinc. The germ portion of the whole wheat grain kernel contains twenty-three nutrients, including protein, essential fatty acids, various vitamins and minerals, as well as significant amounts of B complex vitamins and vitamin E. All germ products should be refrigerated, as the oils they contain make them perishable. Wheat germ can be purchased raw or toasted.

Muesli Muesli is similar to granola in that it is usually a combination of rolled oats coupled with other grains, nuts, seeds, and dried fruits. It is a better choice than granola for most people because it contains minimal if any sweetener.

Oats Steel-cut oats are common to Scottish and Irish oatmeal and are the least processed form of this cereal outside of whole oat groats. Steel-cut oats have been chopped by sharp steel blades to reduce the cereal's normal cooking time from a couple of hours to about forty minutes. Rolled oats, most commonly used for breakfast cereal in the United States, have been softened slightly by steam and then flattened between steel rollers. Oatmeal is a cereal that adds a pleasant chewy texture to breads. Scottish oatmeal is made by crushing groats with stones. It is smaller than steel-cut oats. Quick oats are rolled a little thinner, and instant oatmeal is made paper thin and then dehydrated. Thick rolled oats work better in bread. Oats are a good source of protein, fiber, iron, magnesium, zinc, potassium, manganese, calcium, and copper.

Quinoa Quinoa is an ancient South American grain of pale golden color. It is very high in protein as well as B vitamins, phosphorus, calcium, zinc, and vitamin E. Quinoa flour is now available in natural-food stores.

Wheat berries Wheat berries are the whole, unground kernels of wheat. They are a highly nutritious addition to bread. They are available raw or toasted, as whole kernels or crushed into a very coarse whole wheat flour called cracked wheat.

Wheat bran Wheat bran is the outer layer of the wheat kernel and serves as an excellent source of insoluble fiber.

Leavening Agents

There are a variety of high-quality leavening agents now available that not only affect the physical nature of baked products such as rising and binding but also add nutritional quality.

Baking powder Baking powder is a combination of baking soda and cream of tartar. Double-acting baking powder, the type most commonly available today, uses calcium phosphate and sodium aluminum sulfate as its acids. The term *double-acting* refers to the fact that this powder releases gas twice, once when it comes in contact with moisture and again when heated. Baking powder is used in bread machines only for quick breads.

Baking soda Baking soda is used as a leavening agent in bread baking for quick breads. The alkaline nature of the baking soda reacts with the acid to produce carbon dioxide and is used to neutralize the acidic taste some juices add.

Eggs Eggs act as a leavening agent and binder, giving bread extra lightness, and the yolk imparts a golden color and richness to bread. Real egg bread goes stale within a matter of hours and usually requires oil or butter as a softener. Therefore, fresh homemade egg bread is noticeably softer than store-bought bread. Eggs are not a necessary ingredient but can be used to make a higher protein loaf. An average-size egg contains about 73 percent water, and therefore water measurement should be modified to account for this addition. For each medium-size egg added to a recipe, subtract three tablespoons of liquid.

Egg substitutes Egg substitutes such as Ener-G-Foods' powdered egg substitute are now widely available. These substitutes serve many purposes such as being alternatives to animal products and common allergens and for those avoiding cholesterol. Egg replacers are available as liquid egg substitutes, which are usually made from egg whites, vegetable oils, and thickeners. There are also several powdered egg substitutes on the market, which are usually made from a base of tapioca, potato starch, calcium carbonate, and cellulose.

Sourdough Sourdough is the combination of flour and fermented yeast. Sourdough starter is a necessary ingredient in sourdough baking.

Yeast Yeast, or baker's yeast, is a tiny single-celled organism. It is used as a leavening agent that can be found packaged in three envelopes, in a small solid cake, or in bulk. Refrigeration will extend the shelf life. Yeast feeds on sugar and needs liquid and warmth to function properly. It is inhibited by salt, extreme temperatures, and lack of water. Active dry yeast is simply dried granules of yeast and is the only kind of yeast used in bread machines.

Xanthan gum Xanthan gum powder is a substitute for gluten and is available in most health-food and natural-food stores. It is made from a tiny microorganism called *Xanthomonas campestris* and is composed primarily of carbohydrate.

Miscellaneous

Bean flakes Bean flakes, such as dried black bean or dried pinto bean flakes, can be purchased at health-food stores. They are generally sold as reconstitutable refried beans or dip and serve to add color, flavor, complex carbohydrate, and protein to savory bread recipes.

Caramel coloring Caramel coloring used in commercialized breads is simply burned sugar or caramel syrup. It adds color, moisture, and a slight sweetness to bread. It adds no nutritional value yet makes bread darker, which makes it look like whole wheat bread even though it may not be. Always read the label of store-bought baked products to be sure they are whole grain.

Coffee substitutes Instant coffee substitutes, which can be purchased at most grocery stores, are usually dried grain-based products with sweeteners added. Add a tablespoon or two to your bread recipes to add color and rich sweetening. There are several on the market, for example, Inka and Postum.

Flaxseed Flaxseeds are a rich source of the healthful omega-3 fatty acids and fiber. They can be purchased whole, ground, or in the form of flaxseed oil. Whole seeds add speckles and texture to bread without imparting the fishy flavor that often comes from old flaxseed oil.

Herbs and spices Herbs and spices can be used liberally to flavor a loaf. Fresh herbs can also be substituted for dried ones. Try the following in sweet or savory breads: anise, basil, caraway, cardamom, cilantro, cinnamon, cumin, dill, fennel, oregano, marjoram, mustard, nutmeg, pepper, rosemary, tarragon, or thyme.

Lecithin Lecithin is a phospholipid, also referred to as phosphotidyl choline. It is found in concentration in the oil of egg yolks and soybeans. The addition of lecithin in bread recipes results in a creamy texture. Add one tablespoon of lecithin granules per cup of flour. Soy-extracted lecithin can be purchased as dried granules or in liquid form.

Nuts and seeds Nuts and seeds can be added whole along with other ingredients or ground, chopped, or slivered to the top of the loaf just prior to baking. Nuts and seeds contain natural oils, which go rancid fairly quickly. Rancid oils have an off flavor and less than healthful qualities. Refrigerate or freeze nuts to preserve freshness. Try the following in generous amounts to add healthful oils, concentrated protein, and crunch to your favorite recipes: almonds, brazil nuts, cashews, hazelnuts, macadamia nuts, mixed nuts, peanuts, pecans, pistachios, poppy seeds, pumpkin seeds, sesame seeds, sunflower seeds, or walnuts. Toasting the seeds and nuts will bring out the aroma of their natural oils, giving bread even more flavor.

Potatoes Potatoes can be added to a recipe in mashed, baked, or instant form for breads with a hearty and chewy texture. Potato flour and potato starch flour are available at health-food stores. Potatoes contain concentrated amounts of vitamin C and potassium.

Raisins Raisins are loaded with iron and potassium. They are also a good source of calcium, sodium, and phosphorus. Other dried fruits also work well in bread baking.

Rice polish Rice polish is the meal taken off brown rice in order to make white rice. It is composed mainly of the rice germ and the rice bran. Therefore, it is fiber-rich, high-protein, and a great source of vitamins B-1 and B-3, potassium, and iron. It is gluten free and acceptable for wheat-free or gluten-free diets. Pure rice polish is available through natural products distributors such as Ener-G Foods. (See "Sources for Baking Ingredients" later in this book.)

Salt Salt is a mineral derived from seawater. It functions as a mild yeast inhibitor. Salt adds flavor and acts as a preservative. Remember that there may be hidden salt content in other ingredients such as butter. Salt is the major source of sodium in the American diet. The amount of salt in a recipe can be reduced to whatever your taste buds or doctor dictates. Each teaspoon of salt contains 2000 mg of sodium.

Soy Products

Soymilk   Soybean milk, or soymilk, is a commonly available alternative to cow's milk for those with allergies to milk, or those with lactose intolerance or those just wishing to avoid cholesterol and animal products. Always buy fortified soymilk if you avoid dairy products. It is nutritionally comparable to milk.

Tofu   Tofu is soybean curd and is sold in white rectangular cakes. Soy products are also available as drinks (soymilk) or dried. Tofu is widely available in several forms ranging from silken soft to high-fiber firm. It is revered as a high-quality vegetable protein source. The lecithin content of soy products makes them perfect dough enhancers. When fresh, tofu imparts very little inherent flavor but absorbs spices, herbs, and flavorings well.

Sweeteners

Sweeteners provide distinct flavors to the bread, create tenderness and fineness of texture, retain moisture, help brown the crust, and provide food for the yeast. Sweeteners can be substituted for one another depending on desired flavor.

Brown rice syrup   Brown rice syrup is produced by using malt enzymes to convert the starch in rice into a sweet, thick syrup. The result is a neutral-flavored, mild liquid sweetener.

Brown sugar   Brown sugar is basically refined white cane sugar with molasses added for coloring.

Dates   Dates can be added whole or in pieces to sweeten and flavor breads. Use up to ½ cup for a fragrant, rich, and delicious loaf.

Date sugar   Date sugar is simply finely ground dehydrated dates. Rich in minerals and vitamins, it is a healthful alternative to refined sugars.

Fructose   Fructose is a sweetener extracted from fruits, cane, corn, beets, and honey. It is sold as a powder or a liquid. Fructose powder extract is fairly neutral in flavor and versatile in its use as a cane sugar substitute. It is sweeter than sugar, so less is needed: about one-third the amount will do.

Fruit juice concentrate   Fruit juice concentrate imparts the flavor of the fruit it is made from, such as pineapple, peach, or pear.

Honey   Honey comes in a variety of flavors depending on the type of crop from which the bees gathered their pollen, such as buckwheat, wildflower, clover, orange blossom, or sage. Unfiltered honey contains nutritionally valuable bee pollen. Those suffering from allergies will find filtered honey to be a more pure and less allergenic product. Honey is sweeter than cane sugar, so less is needed. Honey should not be fed to children under one year of age.

Malt   Malt is a derivative of wheat or barley. The whole grain is sprouted, dried, and milled to a fine flour. It is then used as a sweetener and dough enhancer. Barley malt sweetener is made from sprouting, then drying barley grain and finally caramelizing its sugar. Malt is available in powdered or liquid form. It adds a rich and full flavor and is a nutritionally superior sweetener compared with its refined counterparts. Because it is a grain-based sweetener, it is not suitable for those with celiac disease. It is available in health-food stores.

Maple sugar   Maple sugar is maple syrup that has been cooked slowly until dried into granules.

Maple syrup   Maple syrup, the sap of maple trees, has a distinct flavor that adds depth and a rich quality to bread. Purchase pure maple syrup at natural-food stores to avoid brands that may contain residues of chemical extractors. Maple syrup is sweeter than cane sugar and can be substituted at the ratio of two-thirds cup maple syrup to one cup granulated sugar.

Molasses   Molasses is a by-product of sugar production. It adds a dark color and a deep flavor to bread and is a rich source of iron. Just one tablespoon of blackstrap molasses adds five milligrams of iron, which is 33 percent of the RDA.

Sucanat   Sucanat is evaporated cane sugar juice. It is less refined than white or brown sugar and has a higher mineral and vitamin content. This brand of unrefined cane sugar is organically grown and free of additives and preservatives.

Measurement
Equivalents

⅛ cup = 1 oz. = 2 Tbs.
¼ cup = 2 oz. = 4 Tbs.
⅓ cup = 2⅔ oz. = 5⅓ Tbs.
⅜ cup = 3 oz. = ¼ cup + 2 Tbs.
½ cup = 4 oz. = 8 Tbs.
⅝ cup = 5 oz. = ½ cup + 2 Tbs.
⅔ cup = 5⅓ oz. = 10⅔ Tbs.
¾ cup = 6 oz. = 12 Tbs.
⅞ cup = 7 oz. = ¾ cup + 2 Tbs.
1 cup = 8 oz. = 16 Tbs.

1 tsp. = ⅓ Tbs.
1½ tsp. = ½ Tbs.
3 tsp. = 1 Tbs.
4 tsp. = 1⅓ Tbs.

Sources for
Baking Ingredients

Arrowhead Mills
110 South Lawton
Hereford, TX 79045
(806)364-0730
This company sells a variety of whole grain flours, including many of the low-gluten ancient grains.

Birkett Mills
P.O. Box 440
Penn Yan, NY 14527
(315)536-3311
Send or call for a free price list. This mill specializes in buckwheat products, stone-ground flours, and seeds for sprouting.

Bob's Red Mill
Natural Foods Inc.
5209 SE International Way
Milwaukie, OR 97222
(503)654-3215

Send or call for a free catalog. They use biodegradable plastic bags and carry over two hundred products, including xanthan gum, brown rice flour, and many other natural-food grains and flours. They have a wide variety of high-quality products and a knowledgeable staff.

Deer Valley Farm
Box 173
Guilford, NY 13780-0173
(607)764-8556
Manufacturer and supplier of baking supplies such as grains, seeds, cereals, kamut, spelt, quinoa, and spelt breads, and many of their products are organic.

Ener-G Foods, Inc.
P.O. Box 84487
Seattle, WA 98124
(206)767-6660
(800)331-5222
Send or call for a free catalog that lists all of their gluten-free products. They carry a variety of baking products such as xanthan gum, potato flour, egg replacer, and organic flours and grains.

Jaffe Bros., Inc.
P.O. Box 636
Valley Center, CA 92082
(619)749-1133
Fax: (207)785-4907
This firm features a large selection of organic grains, flours, dried fruits, nuts, and seeds.

King Arthur Flour
RR 2, Box 56
Norwich, VT 05055
(800)827-6836
Send or call for a free catalog. This firm carries bulk yeast, spelt flour, quinoa flour, amaranth flour, triticale, soy flour, and barley flour; some of the thirty-five different flours they carry are organic. They also sell bread machines, bread pans, pizza stones, and other bread-baking supplies.

Mountain Ark Trading Company
P.O. Box 3170
Fayetteville, AR 72701
(800)643-8909

Call for a free catalog. This company carries organic whole grains such as amaranth, quinoa, kasha, and rye berries as well as whole grain flours such as spelt, brown teff, and barley.

Niblack Foods, Inc.
900 Jefferson Road, Bldg. 5
Rochester, NY 14623
(716)292-0790
(800)724-8883

This company carries barley malt syrup, xanthan gum, gluten flour, seven-grain cereal, flours, spices, bulk yeast, and caramel coloring.

G. B. Ratto & Co.
821 Washington Street
Oakland, CA 94607
(510)832-6503

Send or call for a free catalog. This firm carries a wide variety of flours and meals, including garbanzo.

The Vermont Country Store
P.O. Box 3000
Manchester Center, VT 05255
(802)362-2400

Send or call for a free catalog. Stone-ground whole grain flours, cornmeal, cereals, and other baking ingredients are available from this firm.

Walnut Acres
Penns Creek, PA 17862
(800)433-3998

Send or call for a free catalog. This company carries a broad range of organic flours, nut butters, fruits, nuts, and other organic whole foods and baking supplies.

War Eagle Mill
Rte. 5, Box 411
Rogers, AR 72756
(501)789-5343

Send or call for a free catalog. This company produces many stone-ground products, including yellow and white cornmeal, cracked wheat, wheat bran, wheat germ, whole wheat flour, buckwheat flour, and rye flour.

INTERNATIONAL CONVERSION CHART

These are not exact equivalents: they have been slightly rounded to make measuring easier.

LIQUID MEASUREMENTS

American	Imperial	Metric	Australian
2 tablespoons (1 oz.)	1 fl. oz.	30 ml	1 tablespoon
¼ cup (2 oz.)	2 fl. oz.	60 ml	2 tablespoons
⅓ cup (3 oz.)	3 fl. oz.	80 ml	¼ cup
½ cup (4 oz.)	4 fl. oz.	125 ml	⅓ cup
⅔ cup (5 oz.)	5 fl. oz.	165 ml	½ cup
¾ cup (6 oz.)	6 fl. oz.	185 ml	⅔ cup
1 cup (8 oz.)	8 fl. oz.	250 ml	¾ cup

SPOON MEASUREMENTS

American	Metric
¼ teaspoon	1 ml
½ teaspoon	2 ml
1 teaspoon	5 ml
1 tablespoon	15 ml

OVEN TEMPERATURES

Fahrenheit	Centigrade	Gas
250	120	½
300	150	2
325	160	3
350	180	4
375	190	5
400	200	6
450	230	8

WEIGHTS

U.S./UK	Metric
1 oz.	30 grams (g)
2 oz.	60 g
4 oz. (¼ lb)	125 g
5 oz. (⅓ lb)	155 g
6 oz.	185 g
7 oz.	220 g
8 oz. (½ lb)	250 g
10 oz.	315 g
12 oz. (¾ lb)	375 g
14 oz.	440 g
16 oz. (1 lb)	500 g
2 lbs.	1 kg

Index

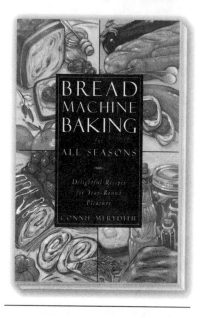

To Order Books

Please send me the following items:

Quantity	Title	Unit Price	Total
_____	Bread Machine Baking for All Seasons	$ _____	$ _____
_____	Miracle Muffins	$ _____	$ _____
_____	The New Complete Book of Bread Machine Baking	$ _____	$ _____
_____	_____	$ _____	$ _____

	Subtotal	$ _____
	7.25% Sales Tax (CA only)	$ _____
	7% Sales Tax (PA only)	$ _____
	5% Sales Tax (IN only)	$ _____
	7% G.S.T. Tax (Canada only)	$ _____
	Priority Shipping	$ _____
	Total Order	$ _____

FREE
Ground Freight in U.S. and Canada

Foreign and all Priority Request orders:
Call Customer Service
for price quote at 916-787-7000

By Telephone: With American Express, MC, or Visa, call 800-632-8676, Monday–Friday, 8:30–4:30.
www.primapublishing.com
By E-mail: sales@primapub.com
By Mail: Just fill out the information below and send with your remittance to:
Prima Publishing ▪ P.O. Box 1260BK ▪ Rocklin, CA 95677

Name _____

Address _____

City _____ State _____ ZIP _____

American Express/MC/Visa# _____ Exp. _____

Check/money order enclosed for $ _____ Payable to Prima Publishing

Daytime telephone _____

Signature _____